Breathe: Run Your Race

Based on a True Story

Sahara Stafford

BookLocker
Trenton, Georgia

Published by BookLocker.com, Inc., Trenton, Georgia, U.S.A.

Printed on acid-free paper.

BookLocker.com, Inc.
2022

This book is dedicated with Love to my daughters Bianca, Michelle and Odette who consistently encouraged and believed in me.

1

Our holiday was fast approaching. Anthony, Robyn, Stephanie, and I set the perfect day for it. We would depart on Friday. I was beyond thrilled and could hardly wait for Friday to come. It had been three years since I'd last taken a trip to the place of my birth. Just two more days to start our journey!

The homestead on the farm was a simple yet comfortable place. The house was surrounded by acres of land that stretched for miles. I sighed with nostalgia as I remembered the fun my siblings and I had growing up in my home town. Megan, Rosemary, and Geraldine were my elder sisters, and Wilfred my eldest brother. The other four brothers were Francis, Hilton, Dave, and Andrew, all older than me. My parents gave us everything we needed, considering that we came from an underprivileged background. It is very difficult to find the right words to describe my parents, though the most fitting that comes to mind is 'old-fashioned', in the sense that 'it has to be done in a certain way; our parents did it like that, and that is the way it will be done'.

My father was a devoted farmer who kept himself occupied, especially if it involved improvements to the farm.

Since there was always some kind of repair needed, he was always very busy. He found work even when family or visitors were around and made sure that the place always looked good. He grew his own food throughout the year, so there was never a shortage of provisions. He kept the orchard well pruned and grew all kinds of fruit—grapes, apples, mangoes, and pears, to name just a few. My father worked until he was exhausted. By the end of the day, he found the nearest couch to put his feet up and took a deserved break.

The best connection I had with my father was when I sat next to him in a small space on the seat of the tractor, into which I fitted perfectly. He would take me for a ride and allow me to turn the steering wheel. It was an incredible experience that left a lasting impression on me.

Then one day he fell ill. He was diagnosed with pancreatic cancer. The news hit the family hard as we tried to make sense of the diagnosis. Many questions were going through our minds. What would happen to my mother? Who would take over the running of the farm? How would my mother live on her own? I was filled with sadness and felt defenceless at the news.

The family was devastated, as my father was only in his early sixties. His health deteriorated rapidly as he desperately battled against the dreaded disease. He became increasingly frailer as his cancer advanced. He passed away a few months later, on a cold December morning. It was the saddest time I can remember in my life. At the time I was not sure whether I was sad for my father passing on or for my mother's loss, but as time went by, I became aware that it was both.

His death was like a blow to my head, which left me feeling empty. It was the first real bereavement we'd experienced. We were miserable as we each grieved for our father, but eventually acceptance followed as the months went by. At the same time, it was very difficult to conceive that he would be absent from us forever. I yearned for just one more opportunity to tell him how happy he'd made me feel as a child. I was filled with so much sorrow that none of it seemed real. I had tormented thoughts of his body lying in the coffin. I could not contain my tears. He was truly the greatest man I had ever known.

My heart ached each time I looked at my mother and thought of how lonely she was going to be. Her life was focused on him. They spent every moment together. He loved my mother completely and with all his heart. It was hard to imagine her alone without my father at her side. Some days would be tougher than others, but with time, she would gain her strength and deal with the unpleasant emotions.

From an early age, my mother imparted wise words to us. She taught us never to be reckless in any of our deeds or actions, especially if intended to hurt someone else. She trained us that every decision or promise we made needed to be premeditated and carefully considered. We learned the value of money from a very young age. My mother was sensitive to all her children. She made time for each one of us. She listened attentively to our stories about our lives and gave us advice suitable for each situation. She always seemed to have the right words no matter the circumstance.

One of the most important lessons she conveyed was that we were to respect the elderly. We learned from our earliest childhood to pray daily. She held Sunday school lessons every week and taught us the lyrics of hymns to sing at church. Her sewing skills were excellent, and she designed all our clothing. She was an amazing woman and was always there

3

when we needed her. Even though her worldly knowledge was limited, she still knew what advice to give each of her children.

Having grown up as the youngest in a large family, I was always taught to listen instead of speaking. I was spoiled by my siblings but especially by my mother. I have fond memories of playing games with my sisters. When I did not win, I sulked, so sometimes they let me win to avoid the kicking and screaming.

My mother often told them to let me win to prevent the tears from falling. There were also the times when my sister Megan and I played with our doll's house, and while we were distracted, my mother put ready-made cakes into our toy oven. All the while, I believed that the cakes were baked in our toy oven. These are among many such fond memories of my childhood.

Two of my elder brothers have passed on. I recall the send-off of one of my brothers as being filled with scandal. His funeral was delayed by almost four hours, during which the mourners became restless, as the corpse had not arrived for the ceremony to take place. The announcement reached us by telephone that his son, Blake had taken control of the hearse with his father's body in the coffin and was driving around looking for narcotics. When they arrived, the driver was beside himself. He reported that Blake had threatened his life and made him drive around until he got his supply—and even made the driver pay for it. The family was astounded by Blake's actions on this day. How could he have driven around with his father's corpse for four hours, knowing that everyone was waiting for the arrival of the body in order for the funeral service to begin? Most of the people present were stunned by the incident, while others were appalled at his behaviour. This fiasco interfered with our ability to deal with the grieving process.

I must say that growing up on the farm was an invaluable gift. It made me truly appreciate life from an early age. Yes, we worked hard on the farm. Our chores were loads more than regular children, but we enjoyed it all. The day I tried to learn to ride a horse I became very excited. I'd watched my siblings riding on horseback, and it looked like a fun experience; however, it also seemed difficult. I remembered standing at the side of the horse when I was little and immediately becoming nervous, as the horse looked huge when I stood next to it. I fell a few times on that day when I first tried to ride and never made an effort to get back on again. My brother Andrew insisted that I *should* get back on, but I simply refused. The instructions my brother gave were too complicated. It just looked too tricky to mount the right way and signal the horse to move correctly. I preferred to ride with someone. The same happened when I learned to ride a bicycle. Sadly, to this day, that anxiety still remains with me. I gave up on attempting either.

Megan and I took endless walks to the forest or to the shop, which was about three miles away. We spoke about anything and everything. We spoke so much on our stroll that we often forgot what my mother had sent us to buy. She firmly sent us back to the shop, obviously telling us a thing or two about being scatterbrained.

I did not realise how homesick I was until now. I had bitter regrets about staying away for such a long time. I really looked forward to returning home. Just the thought of the word 'home' brought excitement to me. Spending time with my family and connecting with them will always bring a fond feeling to me. Our home was always filled with laughter. I missed seeing my loved ones, my sisters and brothers, and the place where I grew up. The thought of seeing my family made my heart soar with gladness. I can honestly say that some of the experiences we gained in the past have been life-changing, and the visit Anthony, Robyn, Stephanie, and I were about to make would be no exception. Apart from the minor arguments that are natural to all big families, the experience was always great.

We led a very protected life. The farm was a quiet place with very little to do during the holidays except visit relatives who stayed nearby, take walks, or read books. During the holiday breaks, we connected with other family members and picnicked on the weekends or camped out near one of the lakes that ran through the farm. We told stories around our campfire at night.

The moonlight reflecting on the lake always looked beautiful as the stars lit up the endless sky above us. The memories that stood out most prominently for me were those from Christmas holidays, when all my brothers and sisters got together to spend quality time at home. Each one brought us gifts, and we sat up chatting into the early hours of the morning. It was customary to listen to Christmas carols, and my brothers loved playing music by Percy Sledge and Frank Sinatra. The tree was decorated by the ladies of the house. There were always stacks of gifts under it. The aromas coming from the kitchen kept everyone around the kitchen table as cakes and all sorts of other baked items came out of the oven.

My brothers collected their bait and spent hours by the lake fishing and having competitions to see who would catch the largest fish. They would bring their catch home for my mother to prepare and cook.

On hot days, we'd all jump into the lake to swim. I loved spending time at the lake. Those were the best recollections for me.

I recall, on one of our walks during our last year of schooling, Megan asking me what I wanted to do in the future. I hadn't given it much thought until that moment. I found the question a little startling. I was uncertain as I thought about her question. On becoming a teenager, I began to feel that the farm life was too lonely. I wanted more. These were life-changing decisions that would affect the rest of my life. I responded that I did not want to spend the rest of my life hidden on the farm. I wanted to make a life on my own. I knew deep in my heart that I wanted a secure future with a fulfilling career. At the same time, I wanted adventure and thought of taking a gap year to decide my career path and to gain insight on what I wanted to do.

Megan and I were lifelong best friends. We discussed many topics, our favourite being the experiences we had at school with our friends or the good-looking guys we admired. We both attended a boarding school and went home during the holidays. My mind drifted to my friend Zoe and her sister, Ann, who were at the same boarding school.

Back then we were not afraid to live on the edge. We behaved in extreme ways, doing things like leaving the school grounds, and that always got us into trouble—until the day we were caught, and there was hell to pay! The mischief was endless, and so was the punishment. We got into serious trouble for our actions, and we were disciplined for not obeying the rules. The day we were caught smoking our parents were called to a meeting, but we were lucky enough to get off with a warning. We learned lesson after lesson at school.

Most of my brothers and sisters had already left home in pursuit of their careers, while others got married. They were spread out around the country and living their own lives. Every memory I had about growing up was very precious to me. My eldest sister, Geraldine, went to varsity to study nursing. She met her lifelong partner and then had two sons. The odds of marriage were against her though, as her partner passed away from cancer. Two of my elder brothers, Francis and Wilfred, were in construction, specialising in building of new homes, doing renovations and other such large projects. I was proud of their achievements.

Megan completed her schooling and ventured into the big city to start her career, leaving me alone at home with my parents to finish high school. She met up with an old flame from school and married him.

A year later, I graduated from school and joined Megan. It was tough when I left home for the first time, as the farm had been my safe place. I lived with Megan for about four months. She helped me to secure a job at a bank. At a later stage, I moved into my own apartment. It was a simple but comfortable one-bedroom dwelling.

Megan had four children—two boys and two girls. Her youngest daughter was born with a malformation. It was a very sad time in our lives and the longest ten months, with continuous hospital visits. One day, the end came for the baby. Megan's was a cry that pierced my heart. I knew immediately that her daughter was gone. Each time when I looked at Megan, I could see the physical pain that had become part of her. A mother burying her child is never easy; it should have been the other way around.

Her daughter should have been crawling around and playing. We prayed for acceptance, and even though she wore a smile on her face, I could sense the hurt she was going through without the presence of her little girl.

I met Anthony on a warm September day. We had mutual friends, and one of them was celebrating a birthday. It was like any other typical Friday night at a bar. He came over to me and introduced himself. We ended up hitting it off. He was different from the other guys I'd met. He had a good sense of humour and made me laugh. He seemed to have all the qualities I was looking for in a partner. He did not hide who he was or pretend to be someone else. He was able to be himself from the beginning. We spoke the whole evening and got along really well. He must have gotten my number from a friend because, a week later, he asked me out on a dinner date. I accepted.

I found him to be a charming person who was always ready to help anyone who needed help. I was happy to be in his company. I later introduced him to my family, who approved of him. He accepted me with my daughter Stephanie, who was a year old when we met. I had a brief relationship that had resulted in me becoming unexpectedly pregnant. Even though his family was not so keen on me, he always stood by me. I could sense the disapproval in his mother's voice when she met me and also thereafter when we had a conversation. But I just brushed it aside, assuring myself that our connection was sure to improve with time.

After dating for a year, Anthony proclaimed to me that he was in love with me. We decided to live together. Our relationship had ups and downs, but we always managed to find ourselves back together and moving on. It made our bond stronger, and we always learnt a lesson from our differences. We celebrated our marriage a year later and had a happy life together; he treated me with great respect.

He made time for all his friends and cultivated a great relationship with them. He held a commendable job in the engineering field, and at a later stage, he developed his career. We moved into a beautiful four-bedroom home with our three daughters—Stephanie, my eldest; Colleen; and Robyn. He was a charming husband and father and treated the children all equally no matter what their circumstances. He laughed a lot and played all sorts of games with the kids. Our home was always filled with friends and family. He took me to exotic restaurants, and we spent lots of quality time together. We made it our priority to go on vacations often and to visit interesting places on these holidays. We genuinely enjoyed each other's company and took an active interest in each other. I surmised our marriage was 'happy ever after' like many marriages I knew of. I was glad to be living in my own fairy tale.

In the interim, I landed a job in the insurance industry. While I was working, I took some courses offered in the company to improve my skills. I obtained a degree in human resources and graduated four years later.

A few years down the line, I opened up a frozen food shop. I knew it was insane at the time, as I did not have any experience running a business and had never owned a business before. Even though I had doubts about myself, I was willing to take the risk. I was confident that it could progress. I armed myself with all the possible knowledge about the business, making sure I was prepared for any pitfalls ahead.

A month after my decision was made, my plans were underway. I found premises and made the necessary renovations to the place so that it would become suitable for the food shop. I appointed an accountant who registered my business with every affiliation where the company was to be registered. She also gave me valuable insights to understand the business world. I became very excited and assured myself that my venture would be successful. I met many other entrepreneurs and was given the opportunity to network with them on a business level and learn from their experiences.

2

My mother fell ill and was hospitalised. She looked frail as we all stood around her bed. It was a stressful time for the family, but we all remained positive as best we could. When she was released from hospital, we spent time with her to celebrate her seventieth birthday. Sadly, she died from a heart condition a few days later, with all her children around her.

What are we going to do without my mother? Could I have done more or spent more time with her while she was alive? I wrestled with my feelings, thinking about her with tears running from my eyes. We were going to miss her greatly, as she had kept our family together. She was our pillar of strength. My parents were our point of stability, but now they were both gone. If only there was a way that we could have saved her, but there was none.

My mother will always have a special place in my heart. I will always treasure the memories of love she lavished on us over the years. I could not imagine that I would not hear her voice again. I hoped to find the strength to get through this heartache. The realisation that we were orphans crept into my mind. It was the emptiest feeling ever. I became an adult orphan with a sense that I belonged to no one. Even though I had known that our parents would not live forever, I was sad for the loss of my mother. One day, I will arrive at a point in my life where I will accept the fact that she is gone. I will remember how lucky I was to have been loved by her.

My brother Hilton took over the running of our family farm, according to our parents' wishes and last instruction. He left his established home to relocate with his family and fulfil my parents' wishes. His marriage took great strain, as his wife was not so keen on the farm life, but she joined him anyway, together with their three children.

The incident stirred up a memory of the day Anthony called me aside. I felt uneasy by the way that he approached me. He sounded very serious when he informed me that the company he worked for had offered him a position to work miles away from home out on site. His salary was adjusted for the period that he worked away from home. In addition, he would come home once a month to be with his family. He went on to say that the company had hired him a one-bedroom flat where he was to reside, with all his expenses paid for. He had already accepted the offer and signed the contract that was presented to him because the offer was too good to refuse. I was taken aback as I still needed his support with the children. I had no car to get around. Nor did I know how to drive.

Two weeks later, he was all packed up and ready to start the journey to his new job. I stood back and watched him get into his car that was packed to the top with all that he needed to make himself comfortable for the duration at work. I was filled with bleakness as I watched him leave, as if we were parting for good. I was devoid of all emotions, speechless for the first time in my life. It was a done deal. I had no choice but to get on with my life. I would have to deal with my three children on my own.

As time went by, the children grew up, left school, went to college, and then started working. My eldest daughter, Stephanie, got married to William. They had four children, two of whom were a set of twins. My two younger daughters, Colleen and Robyn, were still living at home with me. All three were ambitious, and as a result, they were advancing rapidly at their workplaces.

My mind went back to my family vacation. I missed my family. The older I got, the more I realised how much family means, despite any flaws they might have. It was time for a small holiday. I became more excited than ever as I thought about going home. I could not wait to see everybody and just enjoy their presence and be around them. My sister Megan and I went shopping a day before embarking on our trip. As we passed along the shops, I spotted a caravan, with a sign displayed on the door, 'Gypsy — we can read your fortune.' I was curious. I wanted my fortune read.

'You are crazy, Hannah,' said Megan. 'Why do you want to see a gypsy? We are supposed to be shopping for our trip.'

Before we knew it, I was standing in line to have my fortune read. A young woman came out of the caravan and did not agree with her reading from the gypsy. She went on to say, 'This gypsy could not see anything regarding my life in the cards. She suggested that my future is blank and has given me my money back.' She added that she thought the gypsy was a hoax. She ran across the road and entered a shop where an armed robbery was in progress.

I stared in disbelief as four guys with guns pointed them at shoppers in the store. Shots were fired. I then saw the same woman fall to the ground, as she was caught in the crossfire.

Her body lay on the shop floor! I saw shoppers running out of the store. The suspects fled the scene and got away, leaving the girl for dead. The horrific incident took place quickly and in broad daylight with many bewildered onlookers. People were running in all directions. I stood as if I was rooted to the ground. When the crowd rushed to her side, she was already dead.

I could not grasp what had just unfolded before my eyes. Was that why the gypsy had predicted that her future was blank? The commotion was over just as suddenly as it had begun; I was back in the queue, next in line, like nothing had taken place.

I entered the caravan in a trance, as if I were hypnotised, the vision of the woman's lifeless body on the shop floor still imprinted on my mind. The room inside was misty with a sweet smell of burning incense that gave me goosebumps. The fragrance made me feel drowsy. An elderly woman with shining eyes and uncombed grey hair, wearing big gold loop earrings was seated on the floor. She stared at me and then directed me to take a seat on a quaint-looking mat. She placed her deck of tarot cards on a small table before me and then began to speak as she gave me an extensive gaze as if to scrutinise me from head to toe.

'You are a strong, as well as an intelligent woman. You have three children. You are about to undertake a long journey. Be very careful, as I see a bad accident on the road. It is possible that you might not come out of it alive. But if you do, you could be in a wheelchair for the rest of your life. I can see in the cards that you are a Christian. Therefore, your faith, along with your prayers, may just save you.'

She shuffled the cards with her gnarled hands. 'Your husband is a naughty man. Walk around with your eyes open.' She stared at me with those piercing eyes and then continued. 'You see but you don't want to see. There is a woman who your husband is involved with who does not eat the same food as you do. Be very careful of her, as she is a nasty person. You are in danger and a threat to her. Your business is also in trouble,' she concluded.

I got up from the mat, the hairs on my arms stood straight up. My legs were shaking. I was not handling the details well. I was finding it hard to understand the specifics. Time stood still as I tried my best to wrap my wits around this information.

The words kept streaming through my mind. I could not help wondering about the possibilities, as well as the outcome of all this. My reaction was a nervous silence. I was filled with anxiety. Could there be any truth to what she had said? I had never done anything like this before. Megan was correct in saying that this was the craziest thing I'd ever done in my life.

As I walked towards Megan, she took one good look at me, and said that I looked pale like I'd seen a ghost.

'Has the gypsy given you bad news?' she enquired with a grin on her face.

I remained composed as I calmly divulged everything that the gypsy woman had predicted for me.

'I warned you that it was a bad idea. You should have listened to me in the first place instead of following your impulsive instinct.'

I turned to her. 'Why do I suddenly feel reluctant to go home?' I mumbled nervously.

She waved away my concerns. 'Nothing will come to pass, as it is not your belief. She is not God to predict such things in your life. They just go on guesswork, so don't panic. It's more of a moneymaking gimmick. All they do is influence and convince you that they are telling you the truth. It will be good to be home again. Don't let anything dampen your enthusiasm.'

She was trying to reassure me, but I still could not help feeling anxious. The idea that my actions would jinx my journey was distressing, but I silently reprimanded myself for being superstitious.

The following day at work, I related my gypsy saga to Pat, my colleague. She looked very concerned, with a frown on her face. She suggested taking me to see another gypsy who also read fortunes just to be certain that the gypsy's predictions were false, as she sensed the worry in my voice.

Reluctantly, I went with her. The set-up was exactly the same as that of the gypsy woman I had previously seen in the caravan except that this woman hung a cross on her wall.

'Don't be concerned. It's just a second opinion to prove to you that it is all fake,' Pat assured me.

'Don't you get second opinions from doctors?" I giggled uneasily.

'Nevertheless, I'm here. So why not?'

Once again, I was seated on the floor. I struggled to relax and found it hard to concentrate. The walls were closing in on me. Her voice was low as she began to speak and say exactly what the gypsy woman had told me the day before! I was trembling; surely this was just a coincidence? This was not what I'd expected to hear from her. What started out as curiosity had led to feelings of apprehension. She was supposed to be a psychic.

'Enough!' I yelled as I stood up. 'I don't want to hear any more of this garbage.' I refused to give them the satisfaction of seeing me alarmed, at the same time I strained to remain calm. After all, I assured myself, they only went on guesswork, so why was I losing control?

On our drive back to work, I relayed to Pat everything that the woman said to me. I became stressed, as I did not know what to make of it.

'You need to pray, asking God to protect you so that none of what they have foretold materialises,' she said, expressing great concern. This was clearly not what she had expected to hear.

'It won't happen,' I responded. 'I know it will not happen,' I repeated. 'I do pray after all. I don't believe in such customs anyway.' When we arrived at work, I kept myself busy to block out all the disturbing images so that my thoughts did not have to go back to the events of the day.

Regardless, I kept thinking back to the two gypsies' words. Annoyed, I put my hands over my head, asking myself what had possessed me to take part in such a deed. After all, they are glorified fortune tellers trying to make a living.

I could not get over the similarities of both their predictions. How could they say almost the exact same thing without knowing each other? I had faith that none of the strange events that they foretold would become real, I consoled myself.

I did not inform Megan about the visit to the second gypsy. She would definitely have a heart attack. This would have to be my well-kept secret.

Why did I go to the gypsy? I asked myself as I sank down into the nearest chair when I got home that evening. A happy occasion had just turned into a day of despair followed by useless unwanted thoughts. I dismissed all negative concerns.

I could not help but think about the woman mentioned by the gypsy who 'did not eat the same food as me!' I had no idea what the meaning of that phrase meant. Was she a vegetarian? At that moment, I had no explanation. My mind became a blank, but I was not prepared to spend my limited time pondering puzzles that made no sense to me.

Even though I had my doubts about going to the farm, I was confident that the visit with my family would turn out to be a happy occasion. I was not about to let these predictions dishearten me. I continued to look forward to our family get-together.

I began packing my clothes, preparing for the six-hour journey. It was winter, so I packed warm clothes. The last time I'd visited the farm, there'd been lots of changes made by my brother, so I was prepared to expect the unexpected. At the same time, I also hoped that the changes would not be drastic. The sense of being older brought about a feeling of uncertainty. I wondered if I would be able to master what I could in my youth. Would I attempt to ride a horse or explore the mountains the way I use to? All these reservations entered in my mind as I was packing. Obviously, it may not be the same.

Once again, I became excited and overlooked the two gypsies' invented tale. I was eager to see all the modifications that had been made to the farm. This was going to be a valuable weekend. Looking beyond all the uncertainty, I was optimistic that we would have a safe journey and a great weekend ahead. I wanted to be in harmony with myself, even though my thoughts kept drifting back to my confrontation with the gypsy, which made me uneasy. Still, I was determined to enjoy what lay ahead in the coming few days; nothing was about to get me down.

3

The following morning, I woke up with a welcome feeling of inner peace and tranquility. The day we'd been waiting for was finally here. I waited patiently for the rest of the family to slowly roll out of bed. They awoke one by one. We packed our luggage in the car, and then we were ready to start our journey. I was sad to leave Colleen — my second born — behind, as she'd just given birth to a baby girl, Kiara, who was only two weeks old. She was too tiny to undertake a long journey. I experienced feelings of guilt when Colleen waved goodbye, as this was her first baby; she still needed my guidance. Anyway, I would only be gone for five days, I consoled myself.

'Don't worry, Mum. I will manage,' said my daughter, putting on a brave face. She didn't sound very convincing.

Maybe I was leaving her too soon, but I knew that she and baby would be fine, and at the same time, she will bond with her baby daughter. If it was necessary, help was at hand. Her boyfriend and his family were a phone call away if she needed assistance.

The drive to the farm was jolly, filled with singing playing games, listening to music, and watching the scenery. The minibus we travelled in was spacious enough for five adults and four children. Anthony accompanied us, as it was his weekend to be home. Megan and her family followed in their car. We met the other family members at the farm. The excitement in the minibus was the most precious sound to my ears. Anticipation mounted with every mile as the bus wound through the mountains, drawing nearer to the farm.

We stopped at a halfway station, where there was a small animal farm. The children entertained themselves with the animals. They also climbed onto the swings and played for a while. The ostriches and zebras especially intrigued them. I watched as the children placed pieces of bread in their hands for the ostriches to munch. We bought refreshments and stretched our legs for about twenty minutes.

After the brief stop, we continued on our journey. As I looked through my window, I saw the scenery was dry, but still striking. We all loved nature at its best, with the wonderful smell of the fresh air. I looked further up at the rolling mountains that were covered in snow, and the sun's rays were reflecting the most beautiful rainbow colours. I was in harmony with the scenery. We were fortunate enough to catch a glimpse of a few wild animals on the mountains. The children were enthusiastic as their eyes took in all the beautiful landscapes before them. We also came across new, green vegetation and flowers near fresh-water springs. When we crossed the stony mountains, we caught sight of owls perched in a tree, a sight not often seen, as they came out at night.

We passed an isolated farm that featured a tall double-storey building with high fencing. The building gave me the impression that it was abandoned or neglected. Some sections of the structure were roofless and in pieces. The house almost looked like it had become the perfect place for wildlife to make it home. I explained that it was likely a storage building for hay or grain seed or even a livestock barn.

There were great squeals from the children when they saw springboks playfully interacting with one another as if playing a game. We also crossed a few rivers on our journey. The gushing of the water below the car filled the children with excitement. There were monkeys, lots of horses, and other animals to see along the way. They seemed undisturbed by the passing people and cars. They were tolerant of human disturbance and stood calmly chewing the grass that was before them, paying no attention to the commotion or to the people. The kids played games and slept from time to time. They hardly watched any of the movies that we planned for them to view on our journey.

The roads grew narrower as the hills became steeper. I was slightly light-headed as I peeked down the hill. The bus cruised along smoothly as we experienced the spectacular view and appreciated the clear blue sky.

My thoughts went back to the day when Anthony had called me aside to update me that he was going to work away from home. He handed me his contract to read. I remembered holding the papers in my hand for a long time and then handing the contract back to him without reading it. Three children to nurture on my own, I thought then, as I made every effort to digest the information. My youngest child, Robyn, was only seven months old at the time. I had no choice but to play the role of mother and father to my children. A sudden strange wave of despair rushed through my mind as I considered being alone in a big house. All the arrangements were made though. I was not involved; nor was I consulted. 'I am certain that you have weighed the options and made the decision based on what is best for the family,' I responded, trying to remain calm.

He attempted to ease the tension between us by promising to shop for a new vehicle for me once the project was completed. I decided there and then to rise above this situation by turning it into a learning phase for my children and myself. I dispelled the negative thoughts from my mind and ignored the tension that developed between us.

A tap on my shoulder brought me back to reality as the minibus plunged into the driveway leading to the farmhouse. My mind was jolted back to the present. We'd arrived safe and sound and, above all, on schedule. The journey had been long and full of eagerness. The gypsies' fortune telling was fabrication after all. I was safe with a warm feeling that came over me as my feet touched the ground. I was tempted to kiss the flooring as my feet landed. Nothing was about to hold back my enthusiasm for my family visit.

There was a chill in the air, which meant that we could expect a cold weekend ahead. My brother, Hilton, welcomed us with open arms. He was thrilled to see us. He hugged each one of us, and when it came to my turn, he followed his usual habit of tickling me and saying, I've missed you, baby sister.'

'Really, big brother. I think I'm a bit old for this.' I laughed.

'You will never be too old, even when I am a hundred years old and you are eighty; to me, you will always be my little sister.'

The embracing continued until everyone had greeted each other. Everyone was in high spirits. I was delighted to be in my homeland, my safe haven where faces were familiar; the picture had a reassuring effect on me. I was happy to be home. I was filled with regret for staying away for so long. Not much had changed in my absence over the years, though looking around was like seeing certain things for the first time. It was a bit strange to return home, where I'd spent my entire life, the place where I had taken my first footsteps and grown up, but I was very thrilled to be there.

Out of the corner of my eye, I watched as Anthony exchanged his greetings with the family. He seemed preoccupied. I was looking at a stranger. I noticed that he changed more and more with each visit home. He was not the same person I once knew, but I brushed my thoughts aside and continued to embrace the last group of the family that arrived.

We unloaded our luggage from the bus and went into our assigned rooms. We began unpacking and prepared our sleeping areas for the night.

After everyone bathed, we all sat at the table to have dinner. Later, we gathered around the fireplace as each one began to swap stories. Most times, their stories came to life in the form of a scene in a movie as each one gave a dramatised version of his or her experiences, in the hope of making it more exciting. I smiled, savouring the moment as I gazed at each family member, allowing this positive experience to soak into my mind. It was a good feeling to be surrounded by them. There was a lot of laughter as we sat around the fire and watched the flames leaping into the air, anticipating the day ahead. We fed the fire lots of wood, as the unending conversation continued late into the night.

Full of enthusiasm, my nephew Renaldo suggested that we explore the new bridge that was being built over the river that wound through our property into the neighbouring farms.

'It's a huge upgrade as well as a boost to the community. We need to explore to see how far they have progressed,' he proclaimed.

The construction team happened to be two of our relatives, one of whom was my cousin and the other my brother, who were both subcontracted to assist with the structure. As children, we'd crossed the river on horseback. Many people had drowned during the rainy season when the rivers were flooded, so this was a great development for the residents on the farms. In addition, the farmers in the area needed easy access from their farms to the nearby towns, especially those who wanted to move their stock from one property to the next. The bridge had to be strong enough to support heavy loads for the farmers that were moving about on tractors or trucks to cross over.

With that settled, we eagerly looked forward to the next day, as we planned a full day ahead of us with something exciting to do. For the next few hours, everyone was bubbling and pleased with each other's company, as there was still a lot of catching up to do. The farmhouse was flooded with excitement.

Before retiring to bed, I stepped outside for a breath of fresh air with a cup of coffee in my hand. I realised that the time would go by quickly. I did not want my time here to come to an end, so it was essential that I make every second count. I looked up at the heavenly skies that were filled with shining stars. I turned my head. I could almost touch the stars, as they hung so low above me. The view was breathtaking. The farm was the only place I knew where the stars shone so brightly and filled up the sky.

Like any other place, the farm had incurred good and bad memories. The good memories always overpowered the bad.

I began to feel different waves of emotions as I stood in the doorway. I could almost see my mother baking cakes and Christmas pudding. She made sure that each Christmas was special for the family, from the meal to the entertainment. Having a secret Santa was the best experience for the kids. She was filled with humanity and always found ways to enrich people's lives with her kindness.

A typical day on the farm started early in the morning—as soon as the sun began to rise. The boys helped outdoors while the girls stayed behind assisting with the chores in the house. The memory filled me with warmth. I continued to stare at the crystal clear skies. The city with its smog did not give me this view.

My mind kept going back, as if drawn by some worrying thoughts, jumping to the same memory of the day that Anthony left home to go work on site. The days had turned into months. My children had kept me busy with dentist appointments, school meetings, and lots of homework. I'd learnt to cope with the loneliness by keeping busy at work.

To improve the situation at home and make things better for the family, I began to take driving lessons. When Anthony came home on one of his weekend visits, I proudly told him I'd procured a few lessons at the driving school. Instead of having a happy reaction, as I'd expected, he was furious. I couldn't understand his anger, as I would lighten his burden and give him a bit more freedom by doing things for myself rather than waiting for him. But I assumed that he was threatened by my being independent of him. I ignored his reaction and invited him to go for a drive with me so that I could show off my achievement, but it ended in a big fight where he decided to pull up the hand break while I was driving and the car spun around on a busy road. I got out of the car and walked all the way back home. My knees were shaking as I thought of what could have happened to me. At that moment, I realised that he disapproved of my accomplishment.

After a while of him being away from home, I noticed that his attitude towards me changed drastically. He was no longer the same patient person I had once known. Something about him was different. I made every excuse for his actions by blaming the pressure he faced at work. His approach continued to change towards me with each visit home. He became very distant and kept it up for the whole weekend that we were together. When I made a joke, he responded with a forced smile. I tried to hold his hand, but he simply ignored my gesture by walking away.

At breakfast, on one of the weekends that he was home, I enquired what his plans were for the day. He advised me that he was meeting up with a friend. He had not taken me shopping for the necessities that we needed in the home. His time with us was so limited, but he chose to spend that time with a friend instead of with us. He did not consider the fact that I did not own a car; nor did I have anyone to assist me. His behaviour was a little disturbing.

I found it odd that he did not spend as much time as he should have with his children, let alone with me. Did he really think I was foolish enough to believe that he was going to see 'a friend'? It suddenly dawned on me that he found pleasure elsewhere.

The weekend flew by, and then he was all packed up and ready to leave again. We hardly spent any time together. All I'd planned for his weekend visit home went up in smoke. He remained shifty throughout the weekend, avoiding any contact with me.

I continued to stare at the sky. I was taken back to the time when Megan and I had gotten together for one of our sisterly visits. She enquired as to how I was holding out since the last time she'd seen me. I lied, informing her that I was happy, but she did not look convinced by my reply. We continued with our discussion for a while and then went our separate ways. She sensed that I was withdrawn, and I was not myself.

The following week, I went over to Megan's home. I needed a shoulder to cry on.

When I arrived at her place, she looked at me with concern.

'You seem agitated, Hannah. The last time we were together, you were not yourself. Come let's have a drink and catch up,' she said.

A few minutes ticked by. I was totally absorbed in my own thoughts. 'I am fine, just a bit tired,' I lied.

'Are you sure you don't want to talk about it? I have the whole day to listen.'

'I am fine,' I repeated firmly, shaking my head, not really wanting to discuss the topic that was bothering me, hoping that it would go away.

'It can't be that bad. Try me; maybe I can relate to what you are going through.' I just shook my head again, but she was persistent. With tears in my eyes, I eventually started unveiling everything to her, the words came gushing out as I disclosed what was bothering me. 'I hope I am mistaken, but I have a suspicion that Anthony is having an affair. I could be wrong. Deep down in my heart, something tells me that he has met someone.'

'Hell, no!' was Megan's response. 'What makes you say that? *Anthony*, having an affair? I don't think so! He doesn't look like the type that can be unfaithful. Are you sure?' I was silent for a while. *Could it be my imagination? I suppose I could be wrong*, I thought.

'He was unfaithful on two occasions,' I whispered.

'I was pregnant with Colleen when I first noticed his strange behaviour. I suspected that he was having an affair. I was nine months pregnant when he left me at home on the day that you slept over at my house; he spent the weekend with his friend. There were two other women with them. I did approach Anthony. He denied it at first, but when he realised that he was trapped, he offered to tell me the truth. He later boasted that her name was Mercia. He further revealed that he went away to a resort with an old friend of his, Marlon.'

The minutes passed by in distressing silence as Megan absorbed all the information I'd passed on to her.

'Marlon's wife phoned me to confirm my suspicions. I repeated to Anthony that she'd found evidence related to their weekend while she was unpacking Marlon's bags. The evidence proved that they had spent a weekend away with two other women. Marlon could not deny the allegations, as she presented the evidence to him.'

'And when was the second time, Hannah?' asked Megan 'When Robyn was three months old,' I replied, this time with anger. 'He spent the weekend with a woman called Ellen. I later found all the evidence, and when I approached him, he admitted to being unfaithful.' I was emotional as I continued. 'I will never forget that day. It was a Friday evening. I needed a few necessities at home. He took me shopping. He had the audacity to bring her along and introduced her to me as a friend. I kept a discreet eye on them, straining to observe their body language while we were shopping. I believed that she was a friend at the time, but the strange thing is that she and Anthony walked a distance behind deep in conversation, looking very comfortable in each other's company while I did my shopping alone.'

'Why did you not tell me all this before, Hannah?' Megan demanded.

'I never mentioned it before because I thought it was a phase that he was going through. I was hoping for it to stop, but clearly it did not stop. I forgave him for the sake of the children. I have put all my effort into rescuing my marriage, but I am finding it a challenge because I am struggling to forgive him. I'm not sure whether it's worth saving.' I smiled at my sister, but I was very unsettled.

'I will get through this, though,' I stammered. As I glanced at her, she was preoccupied with her own thoughts.

She wore a downcast look on her face, as if trying to make sense of my situation. It was a look that always confused me, and it was difficult to make out what she was thinking about.

'The peculiar thing about it all is that I trusted him. I thought it would fade. I was really naive,' I continued. The truth was not easy to ignore because it hurt so much. I did not want to admit to what was staring me in the face.

Megan had drawn more from me than I'd wanted to reveal.

'Leave him!' she said. 'He does not deserve you. Who does he think he is? He left you at home without a second thought with three children to raise on your own. Robyn was seven months old when he started working away!'

I became uneasy as she expressed her opinion and then began pacing the floor. 'But this time I don't have any tangible proof that he *is* really in a relationship with someone. His actions are telling me something else, but I cannot just go by assumption.'

She remained silent as I made every effort to defend him.

'How can I leave him when I barely make enough on my salary to raise three children? My salary will never get us through the month. I am weak and prone to mistakes like anyone, but none of it is making sense. Maybe I am to blame for all that has happened — '

'Why do you say you are to blame? Did *you* tell him to have an affair?' Megan scolded, filled with aggravation.

'Maybe he doesn't find me attractive anymore. Maybe I'm not what he was looking for in a soulmate,' I responded.

'Stop the maybes! There is nothing wrong with you; perhaps something is wrong with him,' she considered with annoyance.

I could not help but think that working away from home provided him with a perfect cover to conduct his affairs without being seen by prying eyes. I did not expect it to be so hard to talk about. I felt unsafe and raw. I was stripped of my dignity and my self-respect. I wondered if I was hanging onto someone who didn't have an interest in me anymore. Maybe it was the fear of being alone.

I carried on gazing up at the sky. My mind continued to run wild with thoughts that drifted back to the day when I told Anthony about my plans to open my business, but he did not share my enthusiasm.

'What do you know about business? What if you lose all our money?'

I informed him that I would use my money from one of my policies. I refused to have him dishearten me about my plans and took the leap. I vowed not to listen to any negativity and continued with my plans. I employed qualified staff in the relevant fields who trained the less qualified, including myself, as I had no experience. I found the perfect balance between work and my family but devoted most of my time learning to perform each employee's job function.

The shop opened. It all went according to plan. As the days progressed, I managed to grasp as much as I could from all the skilled staff. By the end of the month, I was inspired and was able to perform each job function diligently. This is exactly how I dreamed it ought to be. The work was very fulfilling with continuous challenges and more learning. I was aware that I may face difficulties, but I was prepared to work to make it a success. Though overwhelming at the beginning, business went well. That was enough to put a smile on my face.

My family and friends gave me all the support I needed by pointing me in the right direction. My friend Ann introduced me to a client who required the service I provided. A week later we signed a contract defining our scope of work. I was happy and enjoyed the physical work involved. My business started to grow almost immediately. I began to supply restaurants and other companies with perishables.

After conducting exhaustive research on the market, we were able to identify a gap in the government departments who had no steady supplier of perishable foods. We grabbed the opportunity; it was not long before we started supplying them with all kinds of perishables. My mind was occupied. There was no time to think about Anthony and his infidelity. By now I had become a self-sufficient woman who could stand on my own feet. From the very first month, business went as I predicted. There were slow moments but that was to be expected. I loved what I was doing. My success depended on the uniqueness of our products. I was pleased that I could expand the business by adding new products and hiring more staff, but I really did not want to rush into things too soon. I was pleased with our progress and was also proud of myself with the way the business turned out.

There was still plenty of room for improvement, as we still needed to promote and market the business so it would become known in the field. This was the only way for me to become financially independent. The thought that I could support my family should things go wrong in my marriage, allowed me to look at my financial scenario with ease.

I heard Robyn calling my name and telling me to come to bed. Her voice seemed to be coming from a distance. I snapped out of my thoughts, noticing that my coffee was ice cold. I placed my cup down on the table and gazed at the time. It was way past midnight.

My body rested only four hours that night because my mind had frightening and disturbing thoughts, wondering if my marriage would stand the test of time.

4

After having a large breakfast prepared by the staff, we were off to view the bridge construction site as planned. Indeed, it was as impressive and spectacular as they claimed. The structure looked firm, presenting plenty of safety features. It was an amazing experience to walk over freely with the sound of water flowing below. We strolled to the end of the bridge to get a full view. At the same time, we took in the unlimited beautiful picture of the hills before us. There were lots of people walking, while others were riding bikes. I must say it felt safe being on the bridge; in addition, it was well worth the effort. The bridge filled up with other people who had the same idea as we did.

We stopped from time to time to dip our legs in the water as we walked alongside the river. When we were tired of walking, as well as visiting our favourite childhood spots, it was past midday. We found our preferred private position alongside the river, a short distance away from the bridge. We unpacked our picnic baskets that were prepared for us. We were still keyed up as we all commented on the progress of the bridge. The sound of the calming waters flowing in the river, along with the river eventually having a bridge over it, was pleasing. We stayed on at the site for about three hours and made friends with some of the other holidaymakers as we began discussing the bridge, as well as other general matters.

Eventually, my elder sister Geraldine, Megan, and I went back to the farmhouse to start dinner. We preferred to take a slow walk back. Stephanie; her husband, William; and her sons, Aaron and Cooper, together with Renaldo, my elder sister's son, and Megan's sons, Steven and Ricardo, came too.

Some of the younger generation stayed behind to explore further. They walked along the river's edge and caught some fish. They were not in the least bit ready to go back to the house. Despite the fact that it was winter, the day was warm, and the air was refreshing. There was nothing to change about the day at that moment, as it had turned out to be perfect.

Halfway back to the farmhouse, a man passing by on a tractor trailer stopped to offer us a lift. We were only too glad to accept and climbed onto the trailer, as we were tired from walking for over an hour, and most of the rest of the way was uphill. The kids began to question the safety of the ride, but we convinced them that nothing could possibly go wrong, as this was a small town where everyone knew each other.

We happened to be riding for ten minutes when we heard an unfamiliar grinding noise coming from the engine, like it wanted to stall.

As we got to a steep hill, it stopped. We all waited in anticipation, as the trailer started to roll backwards.

'Something is wrong,' I heard Renaldo announce anxiously.

I was sitting towards the edge of the trailer. I was unable to move forward. As I looked towards the front, I shuddered, sensing that we were in a lot of trouble. I saw smoke coming from the engine. A sudden wave of anxiety attacked me. Every worst possible situation started playing out in my head. Is what I am thinking really about to happen?

By now, the tractor was out of control, making a loud bang as it struck something hard; instead of moving forwards, it continued to move backwards at a rapid speed. A stone that was flung into the air by the wheels hit hard against the side of the tractor, making a deafening sound. Below us was a very steep hill. I started panicking as I looked down that hill. I knew then that we were in great danger and that our lives were at risk.

'Stay calm,' someone whispered.

'It's going to be okay,' someone else reassured us.

It did not seem that way to me. All I saw was my life flashing by before me. I saw the driver wrestle with the big green machine as he was turning the steering wheel in all directions, but the tractor just kept on moving backwards, gathering more speed. The driver managed to stop the tractor from going down the hill by swerving it in the opposite direction. There was a lot of shouting and screaming. I knew something was wrong when I heard all the noise. The tractor came to a standstill.

How could this happen on such a calm road, where we were the only vehicle for miles? It never for one minute occurred to me that we would find ourselves in such a horrific situation, in a village surrounded by solitude, with trees and flowers growing everywhere—a place where the houses were so far apart, there were hardly any cars in sight. How was it possible for an accident to take place in such an isolated location where you seldom see people passing by? Sadly, this was one of those unforeseen freak accidents, an unwanted incident that made me feel powerless to the unexpected traumatic tragedy befalling us.

The last thing I remembered was telling Megan to grab hold of my six-year-old grandson, Aaron. By the time I saw him sliding towards the edge of the trailer, it was already too late to grab him.

I could not reach him. I panicked, as no one was close to him. It all happened so fast.

'Please save him from falling over!' were my last words before I was flung off the back of the tractor's trailer.

I was thrown hard against a rock. I lost consciousness for a short time. When I awoke, I was trapped under the huge back wheel of the tractor, lying face up. I heard Ricardo ask if everyone was safe. The wheel had pinned me to the ground. I was unable to move. I tried to move my head, but I felt a sharp object shift from under the back of my head as if it pierced into my skull. *It must be a stone,* I thought.

'Where is Hannah?' I heard Renaldo's voice at a distance.

Then someone spotted me under the wheel of the tractor. In the midst of my terror, I remember seeing a vision of the gypsy women. I shut my eyes as tightly as I could. Was this the accident they had predicted? There was silence all around as everyone rushed to my side and started assessing my injuries, trying to find a solution on how to get me out from under the big back wheel. There was confusion as everyone tried to offer his or her ideas on how to safely move me out. There was no mistaking the fear in Stephanie and Robyn's voices as they began to scream hysterically when they spotted me.

'Be silent and stop that screaming. You are going to make your mother panic!' I heard Megan's voice command—as if I was not panicking already.

It was then that I observed that I was in big trouble. I could not feel my lower body. I was having difficulty concentrating.

'Take this thing off me!' I screamed at them.

At this stage my body became numb. I was shivering uncontrollably. For an instant, fear spurted through my body as I realised that I could not move my leg, let alone straighten it.

'Help me,' I whispered again. 'Get this thing off me."

Someone took control of the wheel. They managed to start the tractor and drove it off my body. The tractor suddenly started like there was nothing wrong with it. Worst mistake — my body was spun as the wheel skidded off me, taking with it my flesh. There was blood all over.

I could not move at all. I must have slipped into an unconscious state again because, when I opened my eyes, I heard new voices. My body was facing downwards like I'd been turned around.

'We are going to look for help.' I heard the unfamiliar voices coming through as an echo in the background. I suspected that it was the driver and his friend. We expected some assistance from them, but no one returned. We later assumed that they had seen the severity of the accident and had made a decision to make a run for it. My uneasiness intensified as I heard someone trying to evaluate the damage to my leg.

'The flesh on Hannah's leg is shredded and pieces of flesh have been torn from her thigh. Her leg is seriously wounded.'

The rest of the family was notified. They arrived onto the scene. When I opened my eyes and turned my head, I saw terror in their eyes. Something told me that it was worse than I thought.

'The hospital is like three hours away. The ambulance could take up to four hours before it arrives. Hannah's leg does not look good at all!' I heard someone exclaim.

'Hannah is losing blood. We need to act fast and get her to a hospital right away,' said a voice almost in a whisper.

I could not identify any of the people who were speaking. I was petrified as my unmoving body lay at the side of the road trembling with fear. Darkness kept threatening to dominate my senses. My whole body was on fire and was aching like hell.

My family managed to take the seats out of the bus and straightened my leg, easing me onto a home-made stretcher. They laid it flat on the floor of the minibus and then covered me with a blanket. We drove to the nearest town, where we stopped a passing ambulance that was transporting other patients and was going in the opposite direction. They could not help me much, but they did manage to give me morphine for the pain.

Despite being wrapped in a blanket, I was freezing cold and close to tears from the pain. I could feel that my eyes wanted to close; my body was shaking. I just lay there. I could not breathe. The pain shot across my body. *Why me?* I kept asking over and over in my head.

I tried to explain my terror to my sisters, but I also avoided asking how badly my leg was injured, as I did not want to know the extent of my injury at that point.

Geraldine consoled me by declaring that I was a brave person and that I will pull through. Her words did not sound encouraging to me at that particular point. I could not move. Megan told me to close my eyes and concentrate on my breathing but, at the same time, advised me not to fall asleep. How was I supposed to do that? Both my sisters were at the back of the bus with me, doing everything in their power to comfort me. They kept talking to me and gave me water to drink to keep me awake.

'Are you still awake?' whispered Geraldine.

I nodded, unable to speak. I was more aware of the pain in my leg and my back. I moaned in agony. I was getting weaker by the minute. The damage seemed to be more extensive than I believed it to be, as the slightest movement caused me great discomfort. It was an effort to move my body, so I stayed confined to the same sleeping position. My head was pounding, like it was about to explode.

Anthony drove the bus like he was on a racetrack. There was silence as the bus moved forward at an unknown speed, swallowing the kilometers by the minute.

Each time I fell asleep, my sisters gave me a gentle slap in the face to keep me awake. 'Come on now. You cannot sleep. You need to stay awake.'

At one stage, I heard a funny noise coming from the back of the bus. Despite the state that I was in, I asked them to stop to check the back wheel. Anthony pulled off to the side of the road to inspect the wheel.

'We will make it. Nothing major wrong,' I heard Anthony say softly, notifying the co-driver.

It was already night-time when we entered the city. I opened my eyes to see where we were. The lights seemed to have an extra glow, which almost blinded me, while the sound of the cars seemed louder and more deafening than usual. The noise was screaming in my head unlike anything I'd ever heard before. As we passed the tall buildings, they appeared as giants transforming their shapes as they moved about. Maybe I was beginning to hallucinate, as I was feeling feverish and shaky. Suddenly, I became very anxious, not knowing what was happening to me.

We eventually reached the hospital in less than two hours flat. The paramedics rushed to the bus. They lifted me to make me walk. The pain shot through my body like fire. They placed me back in the bus as fast as they had lifted me when they became aware of the severity of the injuries to my leg. I heard one of the paramedics call out for help, stating that I could not walk.

I was strapped on to a stretcher by two medics and then taken to the emergency room. It did not surprise me that I could not walk, as I was unable to feel my limbs. All at once, I was wide awake. I started to panic. I was trembling and experiencing extreme shaking and breathlessness. I uttered a desperate prayer in my heart. I heard many concerned voices. I was afraid as the pain intensified and my anxiety increased. There was a sharp stinging coming from my leg and lower back. It became unbearable as it sliced through my body when they lifted me off the stretcher. I heard one of the nurses in casualty state that my tracksuit was stuck to the flesh of my leg and that they needed to cut the tracksuit pants off. The doctors and nurses were rushing all around me, giving each other instructions. I continued to pray as I held onto my life.

'I am sorry, but you need to leave the room immediately,' the doctor informed my family as he examined me. He looked at them intently and went on to say, 'If you know how to say the *Our Father*, I suggest that you say a lot of them. If you know any other prayers, say them, because she will need them.' Then he continued to administer treatment to me.

What exactly did he mean by that? Why would a doctor make such a statement? I must be in a very critical condition. This must be a mistake. It wasn't supposed to happen like this. But I am alive for now, I reminded myself.

I heard the doctor telling the nurse that I was to be put into a forced coma. I could not grasp the meaning of anyone's words. My thoughts were confused as I had the last flashback of the tractor before my eyes. I could not come to grips with what was happening.

I could not formulate any answers to any of the questions that surfaced to my mind. Maybe some form of shift was about to take place. I imagined myself to be back home sitting in my backyard.

Those were my last thoughts as I drifted into a deep sleep. I was swept away by a calm current, which carried me to the shore. Everything before me began to fade. It became dark as if my brain function was shutting down. All that was taking place around me was beyond my understanding.

5

I sensed that I was being sucked out of my coma. My body was lifted off the bed and then placed on the floor. I sat in a corner my knees bent, listening as voices spoke and people moved about. The voices were muffled, and I could not hear them clearly. I saw two nurses and three strange people standing around my bed. I became nervous. I called out, but there was no response.

I got up from the floor and followed the three strangers, but they just kept walking as if I did not exist. I turned around and saw my body lying on the bed, with many tubes attached to it. My eyes shifted from side to side terrified that they will see me, nonetheless, making an effort to close the distance between us. It was probably the most frightened I've ever been.

I followed the voices for quite a distance. They stopped abruptly, looking in my direction as if they knew I was behind them. As I reached them, they grabbed me and threw me into a train. The train began to move and then accelerate very rapidly as it entered an underground tunnel. It was moving at such a super high speed that I grabbed onto the sides of my seat to keep myself from being flung off.

I heard the screams of the wheels as they made contact with the steel tracks. We sped along faster and faster. As fast as we had accelerated, we began to decelerate and came to an abrupt halt. I was lifted onto my feet and, thereafter, escorted down a passage that led through a building that resembled a bank.

Three gentlemen motioned me forward. One of them held a sharp object to my back. I was petrified and, at the same time, very confused. 'Do as you are told. No one will get hurt.'

Moving forward, I complied and did as I was ordered. They seated me in front of an old gentleman with long white hair, who looked very creepy. I sat straight up before him. He began to speak in a calm tone. He instructed me to sign a piece of paper that he handed to me. I looked around, but nothing was familiar. It appeared that I was in some kind of office.

Once the paper was signed, he signalled to the three men to have me removed as business was concluded. A bag was handed over to the three men, and then we made our way back to the train. They made me walk ahead and followed close behind.

We boarded the train and it began to move. The bag was thrown on the seat opposite of me, where it was unzipped. They sat directly in front of me, and the men began counting the money inside. My face was wet with perspiration as I stared into the stoniest three pairs of eyes I had ever encountered. I looked around, trying to find a way to escape, but there was nothing familiar to me; there was no way out. The minutes ticked by as I prayed for this farce to end.

Once more, the train stopped abruptly. The men thanked me and placed me back on my bed. One of the men told me that Anthony would make sure that the money would be paid back to me. They left holding the bag of money.

What does Anthony have to do with this incident? How is he involved? Where did the money come from? I was filled with uncertainty. I became more disturbed.

I drifted in and out of consciousness. I could feel my bed vibrating. It felt so unsteady that I held on to the rails of the bed. I clenched my sweating fists tightly around them and shut my eyes, half expecting to roll off the bed. I gazed ahead of me, feeling droplets of water over my leg. I strained to see where the water had come from but could not move, as my body felt heavy, as if I was lifting a huge stone.

I was floating above and watched my body as it lay stiff in the bed. I looked on as two nurses entered the room to inspect the bed. They began to murmur under their breaths to each other. I managed to hear one of them say that the bed needed to be fixed before someone senior came back on duty. The other nurse responded that she knew someone who could fix it, but the bed would have to be transported by ambulance.

'We have a serious problem, as the bed is new, and we will be held responsible for the breakage of the bed. This could cost us our jobs,' one of the nurses mumbled in a nervous voice.

I was filled with terror as the side rails of the bed were lifted and wheeled into the ambulance while I still lay in it. My muscles tensed as the ambulance came to a stop. They rolled me out into an open field that looked almost like a sports ground. There was a tree in one of the corners of the field. They began to tie me to the mattress with a thick rope and flung the end of the same rope over the branch of the tree. I was suspended on my mattress in mid-air and looked on as though I was watching a scene from a terrifying movie. Something was out of tune. I could not tell if what was happening was real or not.

As if things were not bad enough, fine raindrops fell on my face. I watched the ambulance, with the two nurses and the broken bed inside, speed off, tearing through the streets with the sirens screaming. They returned sometime later with the repaired automated bed and a bottle of alcohol in their hand. By now the mattress I was tied to was drenched. I was shivering from the cold and exposure.

This is not happening; I must be having delusions.

The nurses lowered me from the tree and placed the damp mattress onto the repaired bed and then wheeled me back into the ambulance. We made our way to the hospital. I found myself back in my room, where they continued their daily duties like nothing out of the ordinary had happened. I was baffled by what had transpired. My fear was on high alert, and I could not put the pieces together. At this point, I was utterly exhausted.

After a long, endless night, it was morning again. I awoke trembling as I heard a woman with a harsh, hoarse voice walk into the ward to address the nurse on duty. 'How is she doing today?' she asked. Her voice seemed to come from the foot of my bed. I heard the shuffling of papers. I could sense that she was uneasy.

Her next statement confirmed my suspicion. She was hesitant, as she lowered her voice while addressing the nurse standing beside my bed. 'I will offer you a large sum of money if you inject this liquid into her drip.' She pointed to a small bottle that she held in her hand and whispered the amount of money into the nurse's ear.

The nurse was silent, as though dumbstruck. The tension between them grew so intense that you could almost cut it with a knife. They began whispering to each other. I could not hear what was being exchanged between the two individuals. I heard a door slam shut, and the woman departed.

She returned later. This time, she was more determined than the first time.

'Has it been done?' she demanded as if she was in a hurry.

'I have no intention of being party to such a hideous crime. If you continue to pursue me, I will report you,' the nurse warned her in a quivering voice.

At that point the woman became hysterical.

'What do you mean *you will not do it*? Are you aware of the position I hold in this hospital? If you object to my order, I will make sure that you lose your job. You will never find work as a nurse in this city again. I know that you drink alcohol on duty. For this reason, I have chosen you.'

I heard the shuffling sound of money being counted.

'Maybe the amount of money is not what you are expecting. I will increase it, but see that the job is done by the time I return.'

By now, my nerves were about to crack. I tried to scream. But my ability to make a sound was zero, and I could not get any words out. I made an attempt to lift myself into a sitting position, but I still could not move. I had a terrifying feeling that someone was holding me down. My heart began to beat rapidly as my breathing increased.

How did I go from being in a hospital to being in a slaughterhouse? Had my family abandoned me? I was ready to explode as my mind went wild with disturbing thoughts.

I must have dozed off, only to be woken up by the unidentified woman's voice. I looked in front of me and noticed that there was a new set of nurses on duty.

'Where is the nurse who was on duty during the day?' she roared. Her voice sounded like a whip cracking in my ear. I could detect her irritation as she spoke.

I tried to make sense of why this person was plotting something so terrible against me. There was a degree of awkwardness as she nervously addressed the nurse.

'Her shift has ended. I am on duty now. She has told me about your intentions, and I've alerted the authorities about your actions. Security will be here soon,' the new nurse standing at my bedside responded.

I remained motionless in my bed and made an effort to stir out of desperation, but I was unable to move or turn. I was trapped in my bed, quivering, as I listened to a soft murmur of voices near me. Once again, the sounds were muffled. I could not make out what was being uttered. I tried to concentrate on the actions at hand.

I heard the door swing open and the sound of distant footsteps retreating in the background as the woman quietly slipped out of the ward, making a quick getaway.

At that pivotal moment, my gut feeling told me that something was not right; this was not the end of her. I couldn't help wondering who the hell this woman was, that had such cruel intentions. *How could she be so icy cold as to go around commanding staff to inject patients with unknown substances – patients who were so feeble and fighting for their lives?* The questions wouldn't stop. *What have I done to her that she wants me dead or whatever it is that she is trying to accomplish?*

All I could do was pray. I was awake most of the night trying to summon the face of the stranger but could not see beyond the nightmare that had just taken place.

I'm sure it will not amount to anything. Maybe this is just a bad dream. I will wake up soon, I eventually consoled myself.

The room became still. I must have fallen asleep again. I was jolted out of my sleep by heavy panting and the sound of four legged animals walking about in the room. I rolled my eyes to my side. I saw two dogs. One was a Rottweiler, and the other a breed unknown to me. The risk of being mauled by these dangerous looking dogs and surviving was slim. *I thought animals were prohibited in the hospital. Who allowed dogs in a ward?*

I directed my attention to the dogs and noticed that one of them was black in colour and had frightening yellow eyes. The other dog was chestnut brown with huge protruding eyes. They were almost as tall as my bed. Their movements suggested that they were provoked or scared, as they restlessly paced the floor.

My body automatically tensed, and the room became extra warm. A frightening feeling came over me, as I still could not shift.

The situation was all-too consuming for me, and I was desperate for answers. My inability to move started to alarm me. I looked to see where the nurses and doctors who were supposed to be on duty had gone. There was no one in sight.

The trauma of the day before came flooding back to me. There was a stabbing pain in my chest with each breath that I took. It felt like I was not getting enough air. Surely someone should be on duty? The dogs continued pacing side by side, their tongues dripping with saliva. I tried to scream to alert someone but in vain. I was still unable to make a sound. Each time the dogs heard a noise outside the door, they began to growl viciously. My eyes caught sight of Robyn and Aaron hiding behind the door. They'd somehow managed to slip into the room. I did not understand what they were doing in the hospital in the early hours of morning. They looked totally petrified by the dogs. I wanted to scream, 'Run!' but still nothing came out of my mouth. Why could nobody hear me?

Fortunately, they had already seen the dogs. As the dogs reached the furthest point from them, I saw them bolt out from behind the door. They ran as fast as they could with the dogs on their heels. They managed to get away to safety, as I heard the quick action of the security guards capturing the dogs. I assumed that they took them out of the hospital.

I shut my eyes and waited for someone to come to my rescue.

'How the hell were two dogs smuggled past security into the wards undetected?' I heard someone enquire.

She must have sneaked them in when no one was in sight, I presumed.

'Forget it. Nothing seems to be working according to plan,' someone moaned. It was the voice of the mysterious woman from the previous day. I shuddered at the sound of it. How did she suddenly reappear on the scene?

'The idea was for the dogs to smell the meat I placed at her bedside and for them to attack her and rip her to pieces, but clearly that did not work. She must have her guardian angel protecting her.' The fury in her voice sounded wicked, and then she stormed out again.

Who was she talking to? I did not see anyone else in the room.

She clearly had every intention of harming me. What had I done to make her so angry that she wanted me out of the way? By now, I was a wreck. It appeared that I was handcuffed to my bed as shock waves rippled through me. She was back!

This time, I identified her by the smell of her perfume as well as the sound of her voice. She was dressed in a nurse's uniform and was accompanied by someone resembling a male doctor who had a stethoscope thrown over his shoulders. Why wasn't I surprised?

Once more, I felt the wetness on my leg, almost like water flowing over it or even as if someone was pressing something cold against my leg. All I could do was lie dead still and remain calm, not that I could move. I kept sliding in and out of this dark place. Why could I not stay focused on the scene before me?

'We can make millions if we pull this one off. Body parts sell very quickly. If we take the kidneys and the heart, we could sell them the same day. I have a very anxious client who is willing to pay my asking price. We can also take all this blood at her bedside, as there is a demand for it,' she murmured to her accomplice.

Did I really hear them say body parts? Are they referring to me? My goodness, it sounded as if they had plans to take my organs while I was still alive!

Alarm bells were sounding again. I was near my breaking point and feared for my life. My sixth sense warned me that something bad was about to happen that I could not avoid.

'Who are you and what are you doing in this ward?' I heard a third voice probing firmly. 'If you do not have any valid identity cards and cannot give a clear explanation of who you are or what business you have in this ward, I will have no choice but to call the authorities. We have been warned to be on the lookout for someone as suspicious-looking as you.'

As I blinked, tears of relief ran down my cheeks, and I let out a sigh of gratitude. I experienced feelings of fear. I lay awake aching for rest, but my mind was wide awake and began to race, trying to figure out how such a confused situation had come about. The machines above me were making loud suctioning sounds that kept me alert. Relief came pouring over me as I drifted into what seemed to be a light sleep.

I was awakened by the sound of the doctor's voice. I concentrated to hear who he was addressing. I was able to discern Anthony's voice. A feeling of comfort and happiness came over me when I heard him speak.

'Thank you very much for meeting me here this morning,' the doctor said. 'I want to take time to discuss your wife's progress with you and the family. Will there be any other family members present at our meeting?' the doctor enquired.

'I will be the only one attending the meeting,' Anthony answered and made an uneasy sound that was familiar to me.

The doctor sounded confused. 'It would benefit the family to know Hannah's progress. I did inform the nurse to instruct everyone beforehand, as this is a very important meeting. It is unusual for the family members not to attend.'

Anthony insisted that he was going to be the only one at the meeting.

'The family previously indicated that they would also like to be present at this meeting and wished to be informed of Hannah's developments. It will be difficult to inform them one by one, especially with a big family such as this,' the doctor persisted.

Just then a phone rang. I heard Anthony answer his phone.

The doctor stepped out, allowing him his privacy while he took his call. 'Don't worry. We will be together soon. She is not going to make it. The most I give her is a day or two, and then it will be over. I will see you over the weekend. I really miss you,' Anthony whispered into his phone.

I was startled and fought to stay awake. I needed to concentrate on what he was saying. I was being let down by the one person I trusted. By now, I was a wreck. My world was turned upside down.

I started to feel hot and cold all at the same time. Our marriage seemed to have run its course. The forces of darkness were upon me. He let me down in my most helpless moment. The betrayal sank in. I was just a problem to him, not a priority.

At this point, the door was flung opened. I heard the voices of Megan and Geraldine.

'You lying, cheating bastard. You have a damn nerve speaking to another woman in the presence of my sister while she is fighting for her life. Geraldine yelled. 'Why did you tell us that the meeting was cancelled? You are playing a dangerous game, you will lose; so if you want to play, let's play!' Megan threatened, unleashing a flurry of unkind words. She was unable to control her temper.

I assumed that they were listening to his conversation from outside the door.

'What the hell are *you* doing here?'

'Stephanie has asked me to attend the meeting in her place, as she does not have the energy to challenge you right now. So here I am,' Megan spat out as she defied Anthony.

He tried to justify himself but sounded guilty as ever. He began to explain his motives and actions. It came to my mind that he was better off remaining silent. *Are you kidding me? Who is going to believe you with all that stuttering and fumbling for words?* I observed.

There was silence as the doctor walked into the ward.

'I am glad you could join us, as what I have to say is of great importance. I know the family is waiting for answers. Hannah is in a very critical condition. It is possible that she may not make it out of her coma alive. We are doing everything that is medically possible to save her, but her chances of survival are poor,' he said, addressing all who were present.

I could hear a smile in Anthony's voice without seeing his face as he questioned the doctor about how soon they'd know for certain whether 'she' would recover.

I did not hear the rest of the discussion, as I was hanging onto the doctor's words – 'she may not make it'.

Why is the doctor saying all of this when I can hear and understand everything he's saying?

I could hear them discussing my fate, and I tried to join in the conversation, but it was hopeless. I listened, and at the same time, I tried my best to make contact – fruitlessly. *Am I about to die?*

'All you can do is pray very hard. I wish it was more positive news, but we are doing our best,' the doctor continued in a sympathetic voice.

The silence was deafening. There were not enough words to describe what I was feeling. I became desperate and disturbed at the conversation between my family and the doctor. It was as if time stood still. My path ahead was unclear. If God made the decision that my life was over, there was nothing I could do to change it; I had to accept my fate. I heard the sound of sniffles. I knew that my sisters were crying about the vulnerability of the situation. *But I am alive. Please hear me, someone. I am alive.*

But my efforts to make contact were futile. The meeting ended. There was a dull silence in the room. The door closed; everyone had left. I was alone with my thoughts. The conversation replayed over and over in my mind. Each time I envisioned the discussion, my panic increased.

I became confused when I heard someone give instructions for my body to be transferred to a mortuary. Dark clouds of mistrust loomed before me. I began to doubt the people who were taking care of me.

Unimaginable as it was, the end had come. From a patient, I became a corpse. I attempted unsuccessfully to lift my arm to get their attention. Conflicting feelings were raging in my mind.

When had the doctors and nurses conducted the physical examination that declared me deceased? I tried to concentrate, but my mind was overthinking.

Before leaving the room, I caught sight of a bird sitting on the windowsill. Somewhere in my mind, I recalled that a bird came with peace, love, and good news. Their presence was associated with good. The sight was comforting. I was determined to stay alive and continue breathing. Surely, they could read my respirations on the machines and see that I was alive?

A small, cold object was slipped under my back. I could not, for the life of me, think what it was. My eyes were closed, and my arms were gently crossed over each other. My body was covered with a sheet and then rolled onto a stretcher in preparation to take me to the mortuary.

At this point, I was silently begging for a meaning to this terrible life-altering moment. I began to argue with God. *How can You let this tragedy happen to me?*

However, I chose to believe that my faith and my trust in God, together with my solid commitment to prayer, would lead someone to my rescue, and it would work out for the best. The ambulance came to a standstill. I was taken into a very cold room and placed on to a table. I could feel the warmth of the blinding bright lights overhead.

'At last, this is the end, and frankly these games were starting to bore me. Did you really think that my plan would be unsuccessful after all the trouble I went to? You were the reason that my relationship with Anthony did not progress. You would not be in this mess if you had acknowledged that he no longer loved you.

Why did you refuse to give him the freedom that he asked for?' said the nameless woman, her pitch angry.

'Pass me the scalpel and let me end this,' she instructed her accomplice. She was impersonating the coroner this time.

God help me! I prayed. I became hysterical, but alas, no one even turned in my direction. Everyone kept ignoring me. Was I invisible?

She was about to make the incision to my collarbone when something vibrated under my back. Just then, I heard the faint sound of a phone ringing, which caught the attention of the other workers, who rushed over to where I was lying.

'I heard a phone ringing. Where is the sound coming from? The sound seems to be coming from underneath the corpse!' someone exclaimed, crying out in surprise.

I felt claustrophobic, along with a tightening in my throat that caused me to cough.

I heard the staff in the morgue shriek in dismay.

'Goodness! Is she still alive?' one of the staff members in the mortuary enquired. 'What in heaven's name is going on here?'

It was at that time that the real coroners walked in and asked, 'Who is this imposter and what is she attempting, impersonating a coroner or doctor?'

The woman tried to explain who she was, but the man in the mortuary grabbed her by the shoulders. She managed to shake off the garment that she was wearing and slipped out of his grasp, making her escape once more. I heard footsteps running in the direction of the exit.

In a flash, the coroner was at my bedside observing my respirations and light reflexes. My wrist was lifted as he checked my pulse to confirm that he could feel a heartbeat. 'How can a mistake like this happen? Who declared this patient dead?'

I had just been spared the ghastly fate of having my body or veins sliced open while I was alive! There were no words to express how afraid I was feeling about my scenario. That day would be etched in my mind for the rest of my life.

I was put back onto the stretcher and wheeled to my ward.

'How could something like this happen?' I heard someone asking incredulously.

'I can't answer that,' was the reply. 'I will accompany the patient to make certain that she reaches her ward safely and, at the same time, open up the necessary investigation reports to verify who pronounced a living patient dead. I need answers, or there will be hell to pay. This is a serious case!'

As I was being taken back to my ward, I perceived that the phone had been slipped under my back by one of the nurses. It must have been the nurse who was providing critical care for me in my ward. She seemed to be aware that I was alive and knew what was transpiring. For some reason, she'd intervened to save my life.

I arrived back in my ward and was put into bed with instructions from the doctor that I was not to be left unattended because of what had taken place. The outcome was all that I hoped for; someone had come, and I had been rescued.

Why would someone want to harm me? Who was it and why? My mind was running wild, and I was helpless, thinking about what might still go wrong.

I slipped into a deep sleep. I was completely alone. There was no sound. Time stood still. Nothing seemed to exist. Nothing was making sense. The past few days felt like a nightmare had unfolded before me. I spent the night wrestling with my thoughts, praying that someone would come to my bedside. I was once more swimming through a muddy tunnel. My life depended on the vigilance of the staff on duty. I was shivering, and my mouth was dry.

My strength and ability to hang on was weakening. My resistance was diminishing. The room became dark, and my eyes became heavy. Then I saw Anthony's mother standing on a hill wearing a red-and-white dress, waving her hands to me.

I waved back and called out to her. 'Go back. Go back home,' she yelled, 'It is not your time yet!' Her voice came across in an echo.

'Time for what?' I asked, twisting and turning in my bed.

'Go back home,' she repeated. 'It is not your time yet. Don't ever tell anyone that you saw me,' she added in a stern voice.

I was puzzled and scared at the same time, but her presence was reassuring. She faded away into the heavens like she was floating in mid-air. I was confused by her message and why she was not walking on the ground. It seemed to me like she had come to tell me that it was not my time to leave this earth yet.

As I turned my head, I noticed that there was an unfamiliar man dressed in a suit standing beside my bed. He started to walk away with his back towards me. I was unable to see his face; I saw the back of his silhouette. Who was he? At this time, I had no answers for all that had occurred.

I thought of my children and my family, and the will to fight returned to me like a flash of lightning. I could hear the humming coming from the machines attached to me. The silence allowed me to listen to the voices in my head.

'Just trust me. I am your strength,' a voice whispered softly in my ear.

I looked ahead, but no one was there. All I needed was peace and serenity to flow through my being.

The minutes ticked by slowly as I remained unmoving in my bed with no sense of time, feeling trapped and unsettled. I listened to my breathing, afraid to sleep, thinking about all the irregular events that had taken place. Somewhere deep in my heart, I knew that God was not done with me yet, because I was alive.

6

I slowly awoke from my drug-induced coma and glanced around at my surroundings. *How did I get here? Where am I?* My mind was unresponsive and could not register as to what was happening, I was confused and lethargic, with little memory of all that had happened.

I recalled having long dreams, more like nightmares, and people speaking to me. I was able to maintain consciousness briefly and was fading in and out of awareness. I became anxious, as everything looked strange. I was finding it hard to concentrate.

I could not explain what I was experiencing as I looked around. Words like 'distressed' and 'overwhelmed' seemed to describe where I was.

Suddenly, I was being lifted and then placed under a tree surrounded by nature, with water flowing below in the river. The tree was soaking up my anxiety, and the soothing sound of the water was transferring peaceful energy into my body, allowing me to calm down. I watched the twigs on the tree sway in the wind. I remained at peace as I waited. The waiting felt like an eternity as I tried to make sense of my confusion and my unknown surroundings.

Then I found myself back in my room. The room had no walls. I could not tell whether I was dreaming or whether it was real. It was dark, and my muscles could not move. Nor could I speak. My vision was hazy, and my body felt like it was floating. As I blinked my eyes, it took a while for them to adjust to the brightness of the light. The mental side effects of not knowing where I was and what was going on were making me go crazy.

I tried to remember something, *anything* that had landed me in this place, but nothing surfaced to my mind. I had no recollection of the past few days. All that had happened to me was a mystery.

If only I could see snapshots of what had occurred to help me understand the last few days; then my memory would be eased.

How long have I been here?

Then it all came flooding back to me. The memory of the accident stood out, imprinted in my mind. I was filled with desperation. The thought that I had nearly died made me frightened to the core. My breathing became shallow. I began to struggle with the images that started flashing before me, like it was happening all over again. *Remain calm*, I told myself. *Am I awake or still asleep? Did I really hear people speaking to me while I was in a coma?*

I made every attempt to understand what had taken place. I tried to place the pieces together. All I could do was wait until someone came to my bedside to shed more light on my situation so that I could restore some sense of control. In the meantime, my mind remained cautious. I resented feeling so incapable and was on the border of going insane.

I could detect a constant, strange smell of gas lingering in the air. The smell seemed very familiar and was prominent. I exerted the energy left in me to remember where that smell came from. There was some emotional connection linking me to the smell. It struck me that I was in a hospital, but it took a while for me to overcome the disorientation. My memory seemed to lapse and then return briefly. All the drainage tubes and pipes were removed. I was terrified, as I knew that I was experiencing moments of sleep paralysis. This could only be due to low oxygen levels in my body that were causing my nightmares and confusion. I was having bad dreams.

There was a sense of relief when the nurse arrived. I relaxed at once as she put many questions to me.

'What is your name? Do you know where you are? How many fingers can you see?'

I answered all her questions correctly.

'Squeeze my hand.'

She had a warm smile on her face as she assured me that I was a brave woman and that I was doing just fine.

After answering all her questions, I developed an unquenchable thirst; my mouth was dry. She began feeding me with ice and apple juice. No matter how much I took in, I still remained thirsty.

I could not get enough. She continued to feed me throughout the day but also indicated that I should slow down, as I had just woken up and that she could not feed me in excess of what was permitted.

I must have swallowed a few litres of ice and apple juice, but it was the most refreshing taste ever.

She sat at my bedside for a while, making sure that I was comfortable. She then proceeded to switch on the television for me. I began to scream at the sight of an ambulance on the screen as I recalled the incident involving the ambulance. Pulses of terror streamed through me, causing me to feel as if I was having an attack. I could not tell what was worse, seeing the ambulance on the television that caused me emotional pain or the fact that I was helpless with the inability to shift in my bed. The walls in the room appeared to be moving and closing in on me. I asked her to switch off the television, which she did.

She glanced at me with an alarmed look. I tried to move my leg, but it felt heavy and inert; my instinct warned me to stay calm.

'Why am I unable to move my leg?' I questioned the nurse.

She answered me with a vague and elusive response, saying that the doctor would explain everything to me in the morning when he made his rounds to all the patients. I was compelled to wait till the morning.

In the meantime, I was very anxious for answers. I was struggling with the fear of having no control of my movements.

I was distressed. My senses were in a hyperactive mode. I tried to avoid any anxiety and remain open-minded as I waited for morning to come, but I could not control my feelings of frustration.

I was hoping to draw some inner strength from somewhere within my reserves.

I must have slept again because as I awoke and opened my eyes, I found Anthony at my bedside. I stared at him uneasily. All the memories of my nightmares came flooding back. I began to scream hysterically.

The nurses came rushing to my side to calm me down and enquire what the cause of my hysterics was. I heard him answer very calmly that everything was in order. They appeared to know who he was and accepted his explanation.

When we were alone, he put the question to me as to why I screamed at the sight of him. I explained about the horrific nightmares I'd suffered while I was in a coma. They seemed to be so genuine that I was unable to draw the line between reality and the nightmares. I had the feeling of being fenced in from all sides, unable to move. I could not make out whether the people who had been talking in my dream were real or not. I became more confused.

My remark seemed to make him uneasy, as he backed down for some unclear reason. I fixed my gaze on him, trying to look for giveaway signs, but none came to light, except for his uneasiness. I also asked him if his mother was still alive. He replied that she'd died a few months ago. He looked confused by my question. It was a relief to establish that it had all been a dream after all.

But which parts were real and why did it all seem so justifiable?

It was evident that the questions in my mind needed answers. I fought against tears of despair that were threatening to reveal my discomfort of being in his presence. Maybe the subject was still too sensitive. He began asking me my name and if I knew where I was and who he was. I remained silent, my mind far away. He asked the questions again. I told him that the nurses had already asked me those questions and that I did know who and where I was.

I had an urge to scream at him in irritation. The physical distance between us grew without him actually taking a step away from me, as I recalled snippets of the meeting with the doctor and my sisters. But I still could not make out which parts were factual. The rest of my family stopped over that evening. They were very excited to find me awake. I listened as they spoke very softly to me and to each other. My family members were gathered in my room. They seemed to understand the pain and anguish I was going through as they stared down at me. I could see the pity in their eyes. I saw a look of helplessness on their faces. I knew that my family had been at my bedside the entire time that I was in a coma, as I remembered hearing their comforting voices.

During their visit, I asked Renaldo to check for leaking gas in my room as I could feel that I was inhaling some sort of a gas that was causing me aggravation. He investigated but found none.

He had a confused look on his face. I insisted that there must be a gas leak coming from the pipes somewhere. To put me at ease, he placed towels under the door. To our relief, I confirmed that I could no longer smell the gas.

Then I began to have flashbacks. Some of the memories of the gas came gushing back to me. It was as if a white cloth was held to my mouth or nose, and my breath was being taken away from me.

The flashback left me as fast as it had come to my mind. My brain was overburdened, as I was trying to make some sense of the terrifying dreams from which I could not escape. I kept hearing voices over and over in my head.

I didn't remember how long I was in a coma, but I was later informed that I had been asleep for about three weeks. My family was very vague, and I could sense that they were feeling awkward and did not want to have the discussion at this point.

It took a few days for me to be fully awake. It felt like I was emerging out of a dark hole. My last memory was when I was in casualty. I was surrounded by hospital staff. There were bright lights shining on me. I remember the bright glow from the lights that kept blinding me, the cutting of my tracksuit, which had all my flesh stuck to it.

When everyone else left the room, Megan and Geraldine stayed behind. They sat at my bedside and then lifted the blankets to see the condition of my leg but could not see a great deal, as my leg was still bandaged.

They related what they knew from the doctors and the reports. They explained that my leg had lost skin, muscles, tissue, and sensation. I learned that 80 per cent of my leg was scarred. The doctor had taken skin from my thigh and grafted it onto my injured leg. He would give me more details when he came to see me. They went on to say that I was very fortunate that all the bones in my leg were intact—not one broken bone. I needed time to digest all this information. They continued to tell me about my leg, but my mind drifted away.

'Will I be able to walk again?' I asked.

'Yes, the doctors say you will walk, but it may take some time.'

'Will I be able to dress as I did previous to the accident?' I asked anxiously.

'For now, it will be better to wear clothes that will cover your leg.'

I sensed that they were uncomfortable on the subject.

Megan went on to say that it was necessary for her to get back home in the coming week to check on her family and to make sure that my family and home were in order. She said her goodbyes and left me to ponder on our discussions.

I could not help but think back to our conversation. I kept visualising the enormous size of the rear wheel of the tractor with my body trapped under it and my desperate attempts to free myself.

I saw everyone standing around me, trying to get the tractor off my body. I had no picture of myself, of what my life would be like, in long pants and long dresses, as my wardrobe consisted mainly of skirts and shorts. My whole closet may possibly have to be changed. I was left feeling sad. I could not glimpse what lay ahead of me. Did this mean that my leg must be permanently covered?

My life was about to take some unknown detour. I was not sure how to process this information. I prayed silently, asking God to make me walk again.

The following morning the doctor walked into my ward with a serious look on his face. He introduced himself as Dr Tyler. He pulled up a chair to sit beside my bed. I stared at him very uneasily. His face looked familiar, but I could not imagine where I'd met him before.

'To say that I am very happy that you are alive is an understatement; you are very lucky to be here, Hannah,' he said, with an almost nervous smile as though to underline what he was saying.

'Luck has nothing to do with it, Doctor. I am blessed,' I Responded.

'Your accident has caused very serious damage to your leg. The tractor caused you to sustain major injuries because of you being trapped under the back wheel and the manner in which the wheel spun off your leg. You have lost 80 per cent of the skin, tissue, and muscles in your left leg. Recovery is going to be slow.

'You will need to be patient throughout your healing process.

You have nerve damage, which is serious; the muscles are going to need a lot of movement in order to heal. The extent of the damage that was done to the nerves and muscles will decide the recovery process. We are hoping for a good recovery. The nerves will repair themselves by growing new nerves and restoring nerve function.

The recovery of muscle function will also occur over a period of time. Exercise will be the key to rebuilding your muscles. We have already performed major reconstructive surgery while you were in a coma and have also done critical skin grafts to your leg.'

I remained silent as he conveyed all the details, trying to absorb everything.

He continued in a determined way and without any interruptions from me. 'The operations you underwent were all successful. In due course, we will perform a few more operations to get the best results on the appearance of your leg.' He explained that the recovery period could take months, and physiotherapy and rehabilitation were required to regain my functions.

'We are not sure at this point whether you will regain sensation back to the leg; only time will tell,' the doctor informed me.

I was too nervous to ask any questions. I forced my mind to concentrate on the present moment, but I could not feel any pain or discomfort, due to medication I was currently taking.

At that point, I noticed that neither of my legs could move.

Was there any more bad news to come? I wondered. The truth was never easy, but at the end of the day, it was better to accept it and deal with it in the best way possible. Right now, was not the time to lose my nerve.

'The process was delayed by a few days because you were a smoker. We were unable to operate on you immediately, as we had to first drain all the fluids from your body through various tubes. We also found water on your lungs, which further delayed the process. You sustained injury to your pelvis and to your back.

No surgery was necessary for the pelvis. Bed rest is all you need while your fracture heals. It will repair of its own accord, and that will take up to six weeks. It is a good thing that your pelvis will heal while you are still bedridden, as you will be here for a while — maybe another eight weeks at most.

'Hannah, do you understand everything I have said? You look a bit pale. You need to get as much rest as you can. I will see you again tomorrow.'

My expectations were shattered as he left me with upsetting thoughts. My heart was pounding from all the information. I was afraid, and all hope left me.

I spent a few more days in ICU and was later transferred into a private ward. I slept most of the day, feeling sad for myself as I endeavored to adapt to my new surroundings. I felt, though, that I would like to look beyond the past events that had taken place and move forward. When I looked back on what had happened, I believed that I had been lifted out of a near-death situation.

For that I was filled with gratitude, even though I kept asking, *why me?*

I started to question my existence — why I was alive — but I knew deep down that God was still guiding me to where I needed to be. No matter how hard this was to deal with, I would fight to overcome the tears and the pain, regardless of my circumstances.

It was crucial for me to pull through, no matter how difficult this whole process was. I will not torment myself by reliving the pain.

I had to let it go even though the discussions were challenging and kept fading in and out of my mind. I was filled with despondent thoughts that kept overpowering me. The accident wiped out all sense of time, which left me in an unimaginable space. Once again, my mind drifted back to that horrible incident. I could hear the tractor being accelerated and moved off my leg. I was shaking as I tried to determine whether there was not any other possible way that the tractor could have been lifted off me, instead of being driven off. But in the moment of terror, all sense was lost.

A *tractor* did all this to me. I began to curse the day of my accident, wondering why life was so unfair to me. My life had gone badly wrong. As soon as I cursed the day, I stopped myself in my tracks, because I knew cursing meant that I was calling bad fortune into my life. Words were like seeds; I was not about to plant bad seeds.

It was of no use to think that far ahead or to fight with myself about the changes that may have to take place. *I will survive the experience, even though it will bring major changes to me*, I reasoned.

I awoke a few mornings later and panicked as I waited the whole of the next day for visitors to arrive. I wondered what had happened to everyone. I was alarmed at the thought of being abandoned and left all on my own. I asked the nurse to switch on the television, as I needed to deal with my fears and keep my mind occupied. I requested that she please let me use her phone to contact my husband and find out why I had no visits from my family that day. I discovered over the phone that visitors were banned for my own protection. Anthony had given the hospital staff strict instructions for me to have no visitors, except for him, and all visitors were to be turned away, especially my family! To make matters worse I was denied any sort of contact with any of my relatives or friends; that meant phone calls and all forms of communication were restricted.

Megan was on her way back home and was already on the freeway when she received a call from my brother Francis, informing her that I was not allowed to have any visitors. He was turned away from my ward at the hospital. Megan panicked and contacted the hospital staff to find out if I had taken a turn for the worse. She wanted to know why I was no longer allowed to have visitors. She was informed by the nurse in charge that Anthony had banned the family from visiting me.

She contacted him immediately and threatened him, telling him to rectify the situation, unless he preferred for her to come all the way back and wanted to face the consequences and the possibility of starting a family feud. She instructed him that he had ten seconds to set the situation right and put an end to all his bullshit.

He tried to justify himself by saying that he did not want anyone coming to the hospital to upset me. She was infuriated by his decision and went absolutely ballistic. My brother was on construction and had come a long way to see me, but because of Anthony's arrangements, the staff refused to allow him into my ward.

How would my brother upset me? I tried to figure this out. *What utter rubbish is going on?*

Once the confusion was sorted out and Anthony lifted the restriction on my visits, my brother was let into the ward. He spent some time with me and reassured me that the situation would be fine, but I could see the concern in his face. The view looked pathetic from where I was and had been blown out of proportion.

My stay at the hospital was miserable and tedious, with continuous fighting between my sisters and Anthony. Lately, they were rubbing each other the wrong way, which caused conflict that was upsetting on both sides. He was demonstrating his anger to the wrong people, as I needed my family at this stage.

I was dismayed by Anthony's lack of discernment when it came to what would benefit my healing.

In the meantime, I continued to heal, but I had no energy or fight left in me. Thinking about these petty fights became exhausting.

My sister-in-law, Olivia, came to bathe me on her lunch break. She massaged me with a home remedy she had prepared, a mixture of oils. She informed me that it had to be done so that I did not develop bedsores and to keep my blood circulating. I sulked because I did not want anyone touching my body and bathing me. The nurses had done enough of that; it made me feel very uncomfortable.

'You need to bathe. Otherwise, you will start breaking out in sores and develop a bad odour. We don't want that to happen to you, do we? How will you feel if your body starts itching? It's not a very comfortable feeling you know,' she explained gently.

I became a bit anxious when I heard her voice. It stirred up my memory of the time that she spent around my bed with a group of people from her church praying for my healing while I was in a coma. It came to mind that, when I could not pray, others had prayed for me, and the power and benefit of prayer had made my healing possible. I was grateful for all who held me in their hearts and in their prayers.

She turned up again the next day with her remedy in hand, this time filled with encouragement. I protested again, but she remained adamant and prepared my bed bath.

'We have to avoid sores at all costs,' she explained.

I eventually relented, and I allowed her to bathe me. I must say that it was a good feeling. She was patient as she massaged me. I suppose stubbornness was to be expected from my side and excused.

Geraldine turned up and had her turn to bathe me, and she also brushed my hair. She brought home-cooked food, but I was unable to eat any of it, as I was battling with my appetite and finding it difficult to swallow the solid food after being fed through a drip for such a long time. Geraldine had nursing experience and was concerned about my lack of appetite. By now, I was being fed solid food but could not swallow any of it. My sense of taste no longer seemed to work as it had before.

'If you don't eat, you will not heal. So, the best thing for you to do is to start eating small portions, unless you want to weaken further and spend a longer time in hospital,' she suggested.

I continued to plead for something soft at all my meals. For the past few days, all I'd managed to eat was yogurt, as eating solid food hurt. Nothing else would go down my throat. This continued for almost two weeks. Lack of appetite seemed to be part of recovering from a coma.

To shy away from all the arguments, I eventually started to eat very small portions as I was advised. I was in no position to argue, as I could feel that my weight and my energy levels had dropped tremendously.

The next day, the doctors gave instructions for physiotherapy to begin and that I should start sitting in a chair for fifteen minutes at a time. The physiotherapy went well, but I was left in tears, as I did not expect my body to be so unresponsive. I was disappointed that I was unable to move my legs in the fashion that I wanted them to move about. I craved being mobile again. I wanted more; maybe it was too soon, but I wanted to be complete.

The nurse lifted me into a sitting position with pillows behind my head. I stared longingly through my window at people walking by in the street. I longed to feel the sun and the wind on my face. I wanted to be free.

During one consultation with the doctor, I asked him if it was possible for me to see a specialist because I was uncomfortable with the swelling that I noticed in my pelvis. He ignored my request and simply proceeded to walk to the next patient, while telling me to consult with Anthony!

'Whatever you need to know, you must address with your husband,' he declared.

I was astounded by his response. I shouted after him to get some clarity, but he just continued walking away to consult the next patient. What was Anthony up to now? He had the audacity to make such decisions without consulting with me first, as this had a direct impact on my well-being. He boldly acted on my behalf without thinking of the consequences his decision might have on me. I was extremely agitated, as he blatantly undermined me. It came down to common courtesy that he should consult me before making a major decision that affected me so seriously or even just give me a heads-up, instead of leaving me in the dark.

I had a right to first-hand information on my treatment. He had domination over my situation, and it was scary.

When Anthony came to see me that evening, I addressed the problem, and I told him what the doctor relayed to me. But he denied having made any agreement of such a nature with the doctors and made excuses for his actions. He was defending himself; damage control was not working for him, as it was clear to see that he was guilty. He was trying to cover up his lies by making himself look innocent. At this, I was afraid of what to expect from Anthony. He seemed to have a hidden agenda, and that agenda was not clear to me.

His manipulating actions were starting to get me down. How could he behave in this manner at such a crucial time? It might even be more practical if he just owned up to his mistake. It could work in his favour, but the lies were causing a trust issue between us. His timing was off, as the swelling on my body needed to be attended to. But right now, I needed permission from him to see a specialist.

My children and grandchildren paid me a visit the following weekend. I was very excited to see them. I asked Colleen whose baby she was taking care of. I could see tears forming in her eyes as she replied that this was her little daughter who had been born three weeks before my accident occurred. I had not recovered my full senses and had no recollection of who she was. I could not explain why I did not know who Kiara was. Nor could I remember anything about her. I observed the confusion between my children; there was silence as they exchanged an uncomfortable look among each other, as if to communicate that something was wrong.

I enquired from them as to why the doctors were discussing my progress and treatments with Anthony and not involving me or updating me about my condition and why was I being overlooked on their morning consultations. They were as surprised and confused as I was. No one could answer my many questions.

When it was time for them to leave, I insisted on walking with them to the door. I expressed that the doctor left instructions that I should start walking. The helpless look showed up in their faces.

They were powerless as they stared at me and explained that I could not walk yet. The visit did not go as effortlessly as I'd hoped. I could see the nervousness in my children's actions.

They tried to restore my confidence, but I remained unsettled, with sorrow wrapping around my heart. I was not in control of my progress, and that resulted in me being in a painful place in my life, which did not sit well with me. Pain had started to become my way of life.

The following weekend, Anthony's family came for the weekend and spent a few hours with me. I was not concerned with the little time they spent with me, as my goal was to regain confidence and get myself well. This was not my finest moment, but when I looked ahead, everything was possible and this unpleasant experience shall pass.

7

nthony strolled into my ward and seated himself on the chair beside my bed. Without warning, he went ahead to give me an update of his intentions to transfer me to a hospital nearer home.

There was something about his approach that set me on edge. He proceeded to tell me that he thought it best for me and the family. He suggested that it would also be easier for the children, as they would be able to see me more frequently and intended to be involved in my progress. He'd made arrangements with our general practitioner, who had already endorsed the necessary preparations for my transfer. The plans were already well underway.

It was senseless to object. *There is no point in disputing the point. He could have prepared me this time around, but once more, it was not important to him.*

'I need to get back to work without further delay, as my company has allocated me special leave for a month. I have already been off work for six weeks. I will be working close to home until you are discharged from hospital. We will depart in three days' time.'

Wow! His plan took shape remarkably fast and was already in motion. I was very nervous about the risks of being moved from a place I had become familiar with to the unknown. But seeing that the move had already been initiated, the sensible thing to do was to be of the same opinion. Besides, my family at home was enthusiastically waiting for my arrival.

'We will use the bus to transport you like before. The seats of the bus have already been removed to make the journey as comfortable as possible. We can lay a mattress on the floor of the bus.' It sounded like he was reciting a poem.

'My brother Shaun has remained behind to assist us on the journey. I have waived the options of an ambulance because of your mental state and the trauma that you have been through; it is advisable to drive down. You are free to reflect on the choices and then decide if you are in agreement with the arrangements,' he continued to brief me on his plans.

I was about to comment when I caught a glimpse of superiority on his face. I, instead, gave him a submissive look of agreement.

I was abashed at my blindness about the situation before me. I needed to put my finger on the bigger picture of what was really happening.

When he left, I thought about it long and hard. I concluded that it *would* probably be for the best for the family and me. The more I thought about it, the more it seemed like the sensible thing to do. I really did miss my children and grandchildren. They had to get back to their homes and respective employments. It was compulsory for the children to return to school, as it was necessary for me to return to my home at some point, whether it was now or tomorrow. *The sooner the better,* I presumed.

It was senseless for me to procrastinate and to run away from the inevitable. After all, it was natural for me to be afraid of leaving the place and the people that I had become comfortable around. Delaying may just bring on new feelings of resentment and cause disagreements that may complicate matters even further.

I did not want to appear dramatic at this stage by postponing what needed to take place eventually. Even though the doctors were not giving me first-hand information about my treatment, I still felt safe being there.

Geraldine almost had a fit when she heard the news of my transfer to another hospital. She enquired as to how I could be moved when my treatment was still in progression. She was determined that I should stay to complete my treatment under the existing doctors.

'This is the most ridiculous thing I have ever heard! You still have a few operations already scheduled,' she protested.

'I know that you might be thinking that the timing is wrong, along with the fact that my treatment is not complete. But due to the circumstances, I do actually feel a longing to be home again, to be nearer to my family. It scares me too to move to another hospital, but I have a longing to be surrounded by my children.'

She succumbed, but was firm about the fact that she did not trust Anthony. My family had repeatedly overheard him speaking on his phone, and judging by his conversations, there was a strong indication that he was seriously involved with another woman.

She was afraid that he may not be committed to me. They also disclosed that Anthony had informed my friends that I would not recover from my coma. He had gone to the lengths of phoning each one of them, even friends that I had not spoken to in ages.

In addition, he'd instructed my accountant to finalise my business and to transfer everything into his name.

Luckily, she, in turn, had contacted my family, who had recommended that she not be hasty but, rather, wait before concluding anything that concerned the business.

This evidence made them afraid of what may possibly happen when I returned home and was put in a vulnerable position. Why did life have to be so complicated? Why did everything have to be analysed? I became very insecure. I could not handle any more battles.

All I wanted was to be at peace and to go back home, where I would be surrounded by a familiar environment. Even though I felt safe here, I also looked forward to being in the presence of my family. I also preferred a new set of doctors to liaise directly with me, unlike the current doctors.

On hearing of my transfer, the doctors were very irritated and lost interest in my progress. They stopped my treatment at once. My leg deteriorated rapidly, like it was starting to decay. I enquired from the nurse what the procedures were when a patient indicated that he or she was considering transferring to another hospital. She responded that the welfare of the patient was no longer the hospital's responsibility. Furthermore, all treatment stopped immediately, which was exactly what had taken place in my case.

I was taken aback by her cold, calculated response. The refusal of treatment was of a serious concern. I still had two days to spend in this hospital. It was the first time I'd heard of such unprofessional hogwash, as I was certain that my medical insurance was covering each day of my stay, together with the treatment at the hospital. The hospital was required to provide treatment that was to my benefit until I was transferred to another hospital.

By late afternoon on the second day, I was feeling a strange sensation in my leg; the stench was getting worse. I was troubled about the unacceptable level of healthcare that was administered to me. This was supposed to be a distinguished hospital. I had serious misgivings about the integrity of the hospital. I lost all faith in the staff that was taking care of me.

When Anthony came to the hospital later that evening, I informed him that the doctors had sidestepped me without consulting with me. I notified him that I suspected that my leg was beginning to have a bad odour.

'Have the doctors said anything to you about stopping my treatment?' I questioned him.

He shook his head in response to my question and informed me that we would be departing shortly. He ignored me and seemed to be annoyed at my prying. 'The doctors on the other side are eagerly awaiting your arrival.' He stood some distance away from me, not even daring to glance in my direction.

'It will be very awkward to travel with this stench coming from my leg. I have addressed the situation with the nurses and the doctors. I have received a negative response.'

He promised to address the problem with the staff. The idea of the move and the fact that I was dependent on him for everything started to scare me. I was unable to help myself at this stage. I was helpless and filled with despair. I was still reliant on the staff to feed me, together with everything else that I required. I lay in bed wide awake and wild with insomnia. I spent the next few hours crying uncontrollably, gazing into space.

I became ambivalent, unable to determine whether I wanted to go or stay. The idea of going to a new environment frightened me.

Everything in me wanted to ignore the doubts that were taunting me, but there was no escaping from them. A decision had to be made. So much had transpired in the last few weeks. I appeared to be on a highly emotional journey that made me feel like I was on a rollercoaster ride. I was unable to differentiate the days of the week, which led me to finding myself spiralling into a dark place with dark thoughts. I prayed that someone would make it right for me and make my world less complicated.

I leaned my self-confidence in God, trusting that something good would come of this. My family came to say their goodbyes that evening, but I could tell from the expression on my sister's face that she was not convinced that this was the right thing that I was doing. Her look said it all. I lay in my bed in a daze, as everything was beginning to get harder to understand. The journey ahead of me seemed to be blank and lengthy.

'I am concerned about your welfare and your ability to adjust to a new hospital and to new doctors,' she said anxiously.

Somehow, I knew from the tone of her voice that there was more than she was letting on.

'It is not safe to travel without qualified staff and without medication. Your leg is still in a critical condition, Hannah.'

'I am aware of the consequences, but Anthony has made all the necessary adjustments for my comfort and safety for travelling. His brother Shaun will be accompanying us on the journey. I would have preferred someone from my family to escort me, but no one was available on those dates. I will be fine; I will find the strength to take on this journey. You can come and see me anytime that you wish to. I have Megan and my kids on that side; they will monitor me. They will keep you updated on all my developments.'

My belongings were all gathered and packed. I was ready for the journey that lay ahead. My mind was made up. I looked forward to leaving the skepticism of the hospital behind and advance into a more beneficial stage of my treatment. It was time to look forward to what lay ahead of me. I would remember the kindness that I received from some of the caregivers in the time that I was at the hospital.

Breathing in the fresh air, seeing the blue sky, and feeling the warmth of the hot sun on my skin was the most soothing sensation I'd felt in a long time. I raised my face to the brightness of the sun and was filled with joy as a gentle breeze came blowing over my face. I turned my head to the side so that I would not be blinded by the sudden glare from the sun. The smell of the ocean, the gushing sound of the waves, and the cries of the seagulls all made me realise how blessed I was to be alive. I was ready for my journey, even though I'd encountered so many tribulations. It was time to erase them from my mind. I was determined to keep going and overcome any resistance.

I was settled into the minibus and made as comfortable as possible. The bus doors closed, and we slowly steered out of the driveway, heading towards home. We drove through tranquil and almost deserted streets with minimum traffic. It was as though the roads were prepared especially for my safety.

The long drive was extremely tiring. But the occasional glimpse of trees and birds flashing by broke the monotony of the purring of the bus engines. Not much was said on the trip, as we were all absorbed in our own thoughts. The odour coming from my leg was becoming unbearable due to the confined space of the bus. I developed a nasty headache from the smell.

I could tell by the expressions on their faces that Anthony and Shaun were experiencing the same discomfort. After a while, Shaun could not bear the smell any longer and covered his nose with the shirt he was wearing. Then later, he asked if there was anything that he could use to relieve the bad smell. The stench was getting worse as we drove along. We started having difficulty with our breathing. There was very little that we could do other than to stop a few times and open the doors wide for the fresh air to circulate. I was extremely embarrassed by the smell that tormented us. I had no control over it. Anthony sounded sincere each time that he asked how I was doing.

It was already late in the evening when we reached our destination. We were relieved when the minibus eventually drove into the hospital driveway. We let out great sighs. We were all thankful that we'd reached the hospital without any medical complications. On arrival, the nurses were waiting to receive me. They helped me out of the bus and onto a stretcher. I was wheeled into my hospital room and then moved onto my bed. I was put into a private ward, since the smell coming from my leg was unbearable.

Anthony and Shaun said their farewells and left the hospital.

'The staff will take good care of you,' Anthony whispered in assurance as he left, promising to be back the following day.

They were probably fatigued from the long uncomfortable drive. I can just imagine the discomfort from the smell, in addition to having to bear it for such an extended period. I was grateful for the care that they'd bestowed on me during the journey.

The doctor on duty examined me to make certain that I was feeling fine. He gave me the necessary medication so that I could make it comfortably through the night.

Nothing more could be done until morning, when the team of doctors would come to consult with me. I eagerly waited for morning to come. Alone once again, I almost dreaded to be left on my own, as I was afraid of my thoughts. *I don't want to be alone.*

I was not ready for the stigma of aloneness in this strange place. It gave me an unsettling feeling of emptiness.

This was not the time for me to fall apart, but a time for me to roll up my sleeves and get rid of all fear and look forward to my gift of healing. I had to be strong; I would not be afraid. I would concentrate on getting well. The tears stung my eyes as the stench from my leg overpowered me. I was afraid to be in this strange place. I felt anxious as the storm of doubt returned. It seemed to take forever for morning to dawn.

8

I was inspired when morning came. The doctors were on schedule and made their rounds early in the morning. The dermatologist introduced himself as Dr Jason. He was accompanied by my new specialist, who introduced himself as Dr Bailey. They explained the way forward in a way that made me feel safe. I was taken into theatre that same morning to have my leg cleaned. The nurse was instructed to remove the pins that had embedded themselves into my new flesh. Many tests and X-rays of my pelvis and back were also taken on that very same day. Examinations were performed, and assessments were made. A thorough check-up from head to toe was conducted, with all procedures being recorded in my file.

The nurses cleaned my wounds. Thereafter, the smell coming from my leg began to ease off. At first, I felt violated as hospital staff took turns to observe my injury. I was totally freaked out as all these new groups of doctors and nurses examined my leg and made comments, while others were sympathising. But as the days went along, I adjusted. I understood that it was necessary for them to familiarise themselves with my condition in order to help me as best they could. I was more comfortable, as they were more professional than my previous doctors had been.

On examination of my catheter, the expression on the doctor's face gave me the indication that it should have been removed a while ago. Somehow in my mind, I imagined that it should have been changed every second week, but I was not sure if it had been done? Maybe it was done while I was asleep, but the discomfort told me something different.

I later discovered that I had picked up a MRSA infection that was particularly dangerous. It was likely caused by the negligence of my previous hospital. I was treated with large doses of antibiotics, as I learned that the infection was life-threatening.

My visitors were instructed to wear disposable gloves, gowns, and masks before entering my ward. I did not grasp the severity of my condition until the nurse informed me that I was lucky that I had not lost my leg.

An intense anger took a hold of me as I thought about my former hospital. It occurred to me that I could have been physically harmed.

'The nurses will do everything they can to make you feel restful. Do not be afraid to call for help at any time,' offered Dr Bailey.

I was happy for the care provided, together with the genuine concern that the doctors and nurses showed. The program arranged for my treatment helped me to adjust, thus falling into a comfortable routine. The storm in my mind subsided. I regained some normality back in my life. The changes had been gradually implemented, making me win back my confidence.

I was happy that my healing process took a turn for the better, with me in the driver's seat controlling my own healthcare and getting answers first-hand. It was satisfying to liaise personally with the doctors. There was an immediate release of the hostility from my previous hospital stay, though there will be times that the traumatic memories will stir up.

Dr Bailey attended to me every day, sometimes twice a day. Before the week ended, he assigned a physiotherapist to teach me various exercises and how to manoeuvre about by myself without the help of the nurses.

At the beginning, I was frustrated, as the progress was slow. I had unrealistic expectations. I needed to allow my body time to heal and face the unexpected illness. As time went on, my frustrations wore off as I began to feel at ease. The threats to my well-being were eliminated, and my struggles were diminishing. I still depended on the nursing staff to help me with all the normal daily activities; with time, I knew that it would improve.

Despite my desperate attempts to deal with my helplessness, I often went into a depressed state.

On one of his morning rounds, Dr Bailey asked if I had seen my leg.

'Not yet,' was my response.

'You are doing very well. I am pleased with your progress, considering the trauma that you have been through. You are fortunate that you lived through such a serious accident. Don't make yourself sad because your leg does not look the way you or other people want it to look. Before you know it, your leg will have grown muscle and flesh. The appearance will improve with time,' he consoled, seeking to pacify me. 'You need to take a look at your leg and come to terms with your injuries. The longer you put it off, the longer you will take to heal emotionally and physically,' he went on.

'Everyone has a battle inside of them. You need to win this battle, Hannah.'

His words had a calming effect on me. However, I could still feel a tinge of anxiety.

The doctor called a nurse to remove the bandages from my leg. My pain was unbearable. The thought of more pain became agonising. I turned my head to look the other way, refusing to face reality. I was not ready for the confrontation and the truth of the disfigurement of my leg. I was gripped by this fear for three days, unable to find the courage to look at my leg. I had so many questions, but there were no answers to all these questions on my mind, instead I was filled with hope for my healing.

A psychologist was called in to assist me on the dilemma I was going through and my inability to face the disfigurement of my leg. On my first visit, she asked me why I thought I needed help and therapy.

'I need someone to help me so that I can deal with the appearance of my leg, someone who will listen and understand the way I feel about the scars on my leg,' I responded, fighting to suppress my tears.

Having the psychologist listen to me and advise me gave me clarity and insight into my situation. On the second visit, I was able to partially deal with my disfigurement. With her help and sincerity, together with the help from the nurses, I decided it was time to face my fears head-on.

The sight that met me was so drastic, I sobbed when I saw the damage that was revealed. I did not recognise my leg. Most of my flesh had been removed. There was hardly any muscle or fat left; it was almost as thin as my arm. It did not look a bit like my other limb. The colour was different too; it attracted attention.

'Don't be afraid, Hannah. You have come through the worst, and you have survived. The process from here forward is reconstructing your leg and coming to terms with what has happened to you.' Dr Bailey tried his best to settle me. How could I accept such a drastic and unattractive change?

My world seemed to be crumbling before my eyes.

When Megan stopped over that evening, she saw that I had been crying; my face was swollen. I showed her my leg, and we both wept. My daughters, Stephanie, Colleen, and Robyn, arrived, and the tears of despair started afresh. Each one took a turn to look at my leg. They were taken aback at the sight, and their expressions of disbelief told me all that I needed to know.

When they left that evening, I prayed like never before. *Please, God, why did this happen to me?* I kept pleading over and over in my head. I called God's name what seemed to be a million times.

All kinds of prayers were going through my mind, but I could only remember a fraction of them. It was difficult thinking about everyone's reaction, which caused all the uncertainties to swirl around in my head. I wanted to know how everything would fall into place. Unfortunately, I could not see beyond what was in front of me.

I considered that I needed to mentally prepare myself for prolonged unpleasant experiences ahead. I had to psychologically force myself to deal with the imperfection of my leg. My life would change dramatically. However, the fact that I had not lost my leg totally motivated me to look forward to learning how to walk independently again. I had a choice — to feel discouraged or to simply accept it for what it was. I could not change anything for now, but at the same time, I was not sure if it was permanent or not. It was of no use to dwell on something that could not be changed. Even though the doctors informed me that I would walk again, it was impossible to see that far ahead.

My healing progress began. I gradually got stronger. I started to relearn how to walk. I was able to accomplish the distance from my bed to the door. Even though it was a very small distance, sometimes I only made it halfway, which was only two to three steps. But I perceived that I had achieved the world.

I wanted to do this for myself, as I was tired of being confined to this one room. Due to my injuries being so severe, relearning to sit and balance was taxing on me and took a lot of my energy.

There were times when I imagined that I was falling. I would start to lose my nerve and want to quit. The loss of sensation in my leg made it difficult for me to hold my body steady and balance myself. Learning to move safely from my bed to a chair as the doctors advised was my main focus. A rehabilitation program was designed by my physiotherapist, which included goals to become independent.

'Beautifully done; see you same time tomorrow,' my physiotherapist encouraged me.

The cheer made my day, and I was pleased with myself.

The hospital staff also inspired me every day by exclaiming, 'Well done, Hannah. You are coming along very well!'

Those moments of tolerance set me free, helping me regain my sense of self-worth and giving me a sense of purpose. It was time to rise to the challenge. The insidious belief of failure left my mind and was thrown to the winds. My inner belief reminded me that I deserved the best in my life, and that belief aided me in avoiding any depressing thoughts that could cause me to break down. God provided me with strength and acceptance in the messiest time of my life.

I made many friends during my stay at the hospital. I was given preferential treatment over the other patients as I had outstayed most of them. It was like being the 'teacher's pet'. I was very grateful for all they'd done for me. The nurses often spent their breaks with me, and we developed a great nurse-patient relationship.

I specially became friends with two of my favourite nurses, Abigail and Mary, who spent extra time with me and showered me with special attention, taking turns to pamper me. At night-time, they waited for everyone to fall asleep, and then they bathed me, brushed my hair, and massaged me from head to toe. We sat up speaking till the early hours of the morning, exchanging our life stories. We watched programs on television when all the patients were settled, and no one senior was around.

During one of my conversations with Mary, I described my disturbing nightmares that kept unsettling me. I informed her that I was afraid they might possibly affect my recovery. The nightmares kept recurring more frequently. At times, they were so intense and disturbing that I found myself feeling faint and breaking out into cold sweats. I also pointed out to her that I remembered speaking to the hospital staff and saying weird things to them. Sometimes I was afraid to sleep because the nightmares felt so close to reality.

She stared at me for a moment and explained that I was very lucky to be alive because, in most cases when dreams of that nature take place, the patient is beyond any hope of recovery. I was very uncomfortable by her information and started jumping to unnecessary conclusions.

'Don't forget to pray, Hannah,' Mary recommended as she quickly slipped away, I think as a means of warding off any more questions. She moved on to do her rounds with the other patients.

'Yes, I will,' I whispered under my breath, with a guilty conscience. *When last did I pray?* I asked myself.

Since my accident and Anthony's affairs, I'd lost the urge to pray, as I was resentful; although fortunately for me, I did not stop altogether. I still could not get myself to pray as often as I should. Instead, I found myself praying when I was in need or when things were going wrong. I was at a point in my life where I was impatient because I did not see immediate results. I wanted answers, like yesterday. My spiritual journey was challenged, I spent most of my spare and alone time wrestling with God about all my disappointments and my expectations. My comfortable world had been shaken, and so had my faith. I had to redevelop my faith and overcome my setbacks.

On one of Dr Bailey's consultations, he informed me that, if I continued doing so well, I could go home soon.

'No, please,' I protested. 'I *really* don't think I am ready to leave the hospital, Doctor,' I pleaded.

He cleared his throat and looked very surprised. He stared at me for a while and then pulled out the chair beside my bed and seated himself next to me. 'You cannot stay here indefinitely and hide from your fears forever, you know. You need to get out there and reclaim your life. It's time to face the world again. You also have to consider that your family needs you. We will meet every four weeks for your appointments and check-ups. We can discuss any problems that arise as well as your progress,' he said persuasively.

'We are very pleased with your recovery and your response to treatment. You are determined, and you stayed motivated. So, continue to strive towards your healing. Your healthy mindset has been the key element to your healing,' he encouraged.

'Soon you will be able to walk, and you will gain your mobility back. You will also be independent once you start walking. That will be a great achievement for you and good reason for you to work very hard towards that goal. It will take some time, but you are a fighter. Abide by my instructions and continue exercising with the physiotherapist as she suggests. You won't be disappointed. The way forward can only be positive.'

We also discussed reconstruction that would be done at a later stage. It was empowering to believe that I had come this far. Even though I was pessimistic, my body had an amazing ability to repair itself. The power of my recovery was nothing short of a miracle. I was surprised at my body's capacity to bounce back from the injuries that I'd sustained, as three weeks ago, I had not foreseen my recovery strengthening and my confidence increasing. My endurance paid off, aided by the grace and mercy of God.

'A home nurse will be making a house call every second day to clean your wounds on your leg and change your dressings. We will be expecting to see you three times a week to continue with physiotherapy. Dr Jason and I have consented that you are ready to be discharged. You can go home by the end of the week. It will be a strain in the beginning, but you will learn to adjust.'

I turned my face away and continued to sulk, not uttering a word. When the doctor left the ward, I stared into space in total confusion. I was afraid. I started imagining many disasters ahead of me. I slept all day, trying to escape any confrontations. I was not ready to go back home; the way forward frightened me. I once more reflected on my impairment, especially the restrictions, the inability to walk, and the clothes that I would have to wear.

Thinking about my marriage and my children scared me, as I felt estranged from my family. I had not been home in over two months and wondered how my family would respond to me with the situation being reversed, with them having to look after me. How would my friends respond when they saw my leg? I didn't want anyone to see me like this. I wanted to be accepted. I wished looks did not matter, but I knew to a certain degree that appearances play an important part in our society. Having so much to deal with at once became devastating. I was without hope. The anxiety caused my feelings to reel out of control.

Then I decided that, even though the painful events of my life lingered in the back of my mind, I could not allow them to consume me. It was not in my blood to give up or to be discouraged.

I made up my mind that it was time to stop focusing on the past and to plan on how to improve my future. That is why it is called the past—it is over; it is history. I had to let it go, since pain and anger would hold me back.

I lay awake long after all my visitors had left that evening. I withdrew into solitude, not wanting to converse with or see anyone. I wanted to stay in the world I had become comfortable in. I wanted to stay right here in the hospital, where I did not have to deal with too many complications and where the nurses were at my disposal.

I was attached to the people who were nursing me. I found it emotionally challenging to be leaving them behind and taking the risk of venturing out. This had become my daily existence. I thought about the painful incidents that marked my life. I did not expect that it would be easy. Tomorrow is not guaranteed, so I will count my blessings as each day is a gift. I knew that my burdens would become lighter as time went by, and that my mind will eventually be calm.

A member from my church dropped by on Sunday morning. It yet again occurred to me that I had not been praying daily as I should have been. She spent some time at my bedside reading passages from the Bible to me. She left me with pamphlets with prayers to give me self-confidence, as well as prayers to guide me along as I prayed daily.

After she departed, I resolved that, as I said the prayers she left behind, they had a significant meaning to my present situation. It became clear to me that God was giving me the strength I needed.

He was with me in the process of my healing. The time we shared was a heartfelt reminder that prayers play an important part of our everyday life. Yet, even though I prayed, I was still filled with anger.

However, with enough prayer and self-discipline, I would pull through and get beyond this bad patch. I was thankful for the fact that I was breathing. I needed to get rid of this nasty irritation I was feeling. I was not about to let this moment of hostility limit my dreams and rob me of the good healing ahead of me. I would do everything—no matter how hard it was—to help myself to advance beyond the bounds and probabilities.

I believe that, by being weak, I became strong. I managed to gain strength to handle what I thought was unattainable. Life does not make sense. Nor does it add up. But after reading the pamphlets given to me, I was given the wisdom to see the hopeful side of my situation and also the encouragement that I needed to persist.

9

Days went by. All my days were pretty busy with either exercise or taking a few extra steps. My recovery continued to be satisfactory.

Sooner than expected, it was my day to be discharged. With the help of Abigail, I once again gathered the small items I'd accumulated. I was all ready and packed for my trip home. It occurred to me that Anthony would fetch me from the hospital, but it turned out that he could not get time off from work, as he was busy. I was upset, as I'd hoped that he would be the one to take me home, but I accepted the fact that he was busy.

My medication was handed to me by the nurse in charge with all the instructions on the dosage and times of use.

Stephanie and Megan arrived to take me home. The attendant wheeled me out of the hospital, and Stephanie carried my bag. She placed it into the boot of the car. When I was settled in my seat and strapped in, we headed home.

We were greeted by pleasant afternoon weather with a soft gentle breeze. The smell of new green leaves sprouting everywhere on the trees announced that it was spring. I appreciated the unlimited beauty of nature that captured me, plus the warmth of the sun on my skin.

While the car was in motion, I caught sight of my leg. I tried to shift it gently to see if it was likely to move, but it did not respond. To my surprise, I did not panic. Nor was I distressed, which brought a smile to my face. I believe that I was beginning to accept my plight.

On arrival home, I was tired and asked my daughter to take me straight to my room. It was weird to be home. I looked around. Some of the items in the house did not seem familiar to me. My daughters carried me to my bedroom, as I was still afraid to walk on my crutches. Each time I tried to move about with them, I had the feeling that I was going to fall to the ground. I grew to be unstable and dreaded the idea of walking with them.

I was entering an entirely new world, as the limitations imposed by the crutches were tough. Adjusting to my new life was a difficult transition, as my plans for my future had to change. Each time I caught a glimpse of my leg, it set off an avalanche of emotions that my scar represented.

Facing the reality that this disability could possibly be with me for a while, I tried to accept my destiny and practiced walking with the crutches every minute that I could. I was determined to get back my freedom to walk again. The idea of venturing out in public terrified me. It was going to be difficult, but I would defeat this challenge because there was no time to quit. The thought did make me feel awkward though, as I knew people undoubtedly would turn their heads to stare at me. Besides the crutches would make them feel sorry for me. I didn't want people to see me this way.

A sense of rejection settled over me as I thought about these facts. I held onto my dream to be mobile. It was wiser to forget about how others would look at me and just have confidence in using the crutches. This was just a small speed bump that I would overcome with time. I believed I could do this because I was not alone. There was still much ahead of me, and some things needed to be left to unravel in their own way at their own time. I wished I knew all the answers, but my life remained a mystery for now. I could not help thinking how blessed people were that they could walk freely. I was sure they didn't even consider it or give it a second thought. I myself had not appreciated the value of my legs until now. Being deeply appreciative that my disability was temporary made me have a different point of view on what those with challenges of a permanent disability must face every day of their lives. I started to look at them in a special way, with utmost respect and admiration.

Watching others in shorts and displaying their legs made me envious, but my turn would come to dress the way it suited me. I made a conscious decision to let nothing hold me back, not even style or fashion.

My loneliness over the next few days plagued me. I had been surrounded by people at the hospital, but at home, the absence of everyone made me withdraw into a shell. My life stood still, with no one to talk to or share my concerns with. The reality of how severe my injury truly was, hit me hard every time I was alone, and that made me sensitive.

The first few weeks of being home were difficult. I found it tough to get into a routine. I was stuck at home on the couch day in and day out, while everyone was at work, and the kids were at school.

When Anthony arrived home that evening, very few words were exchanged between us at the dinner table. Colleen prepared dinner, but I was feeling too gloomy to eat and tossed my food around in my plate. During dinner, he asked how I was feeling but he did not wait for me to respond. When the meal was over, he went straight to bed. It was obvious to me that his thoughts seemed preoccupied. I was more upset than usual by his attitude.

My heart ached at the thought of Anthony philandering with other women.

A flashback moment surfaced to the first time we met. He was a different person at the time. He was compassionate and attentive back then. Those were the times of laughter and joy.

An aching feeling of unhappiness came over me as I thought of the sudden change in his attitude. How could life have dealt me such a cruel blow? Why, at a time when I was vulnerable, did I not have a loving partner to face my challenges with me? What did the future hold for me? An uneasy feeling came over me as all these questions started popping into my mind.

As soon as my health was restored, I vowed to look for any evidence that could explain the change in him. Something didn't feel right, and my gut feeling was telling me to dig for confirmation. Unfortunately, his conduct was leading me to be suspicious. For now, *I* was all that mattered. My healing was my priority. My mind had to become balanced so that my plan of action could be determined.

Colleen and Robyn carried me to my bed once more, as I was still nervous to use my crutches up the stairs. I was afraid to go to bed before Anthony, after he kicked the frame that was protecting my leg from the heaviness of the covers on the bed. The pain was so extreme, it felt like I had bumped my toe against the corner of something, and I burst into tears.

Megan had stopped over that night, and once more, a terrible fight had broken out between her and Anthony. Her vocabulary was very expressive that day as she screamed at the top of her voice. Overcome with exhaustion as I was, sleep still evaded me.

I was restless, with so much going through my mind. Thinking about the continuous conflict between Anthony and Megan was upsetting.

I must have dozed off during the early hours of the morning, for when the sun shone brightly through my window marking the beginning of a brand-new day, it was as if I had not slept at all.

Although later, I did feel what a marvel it was waking up to spend the day sitting outside on my patio, benefiting from the fresh air, and soaking up the sunlight. I was blessed beyond measure but was also so preoccupied with my problems that I often lost sight of the important things in life. The fact kept hitting me that I'd almost lost my life; this made me reassess my priorities.

Later in the day, two of my colleagues stopped over to see me. I was happy to be in their company after such a long time. They had endless questions and updated me on the progress in the shop. Pat had faithfully taken over the running of the business. I missed their companionship very much. I valued having them on board working for me. When Pat asked to see my leg, I was able to show it to her, as I was no longer haunted by the anxiety that I first experienced.

'Oh my goodness, Hannah!' she exclaimed with a look of horror on her face. She burst into tears, covered her face with her hands and ran out of my room.

Reality once more hit me in the face as I witnessed Pat's reaction to seeing my leg. *Will everyone react in this way?*

'You should have cancelled your trip,' she sobbed when she came back. She was a dramatic individual; her reaction was just as I expected it.

'If it was meant to happen to me, it would have happened wherever I was at that moment. It could have happened while I was walking, maybe in a different way. Everything in life occurs for a reason. No amount of safety measures could have prevented it from happening to me. This was apparently my destiny,' I explained to her.

Observing the reaction of my friends as they caught sight of my leg was going to be depressing for me. The rest of the visit was a bit strained, but surprisingly, I was calm and managed to have a smile on my face throughout. Though, on a few occasions the tears threatened, I had to stifle my emotions.

Alone again, even though I was unable to move about and felt useless, I was glad to be given a second chance, as not everyone is that fortunate. I was not about to throw my fortune away. The nurse arrived to clean the wounds on my leg. I took my medication and did my daily exercises regularly. This turned out to be my routine.

I was home two weeks when I noticed a swelling in both my legs. I became alarmed at the size of my feet. I could hardly see my ankles because of how swollen they were. They grew heavy and uncomfortable. I struggled to move them about. Each time I glanced at my feet, they seemed to be swelling even more. My body became cold. I kept asking to be covered with more blankets.

Megan popped by that morning. She and Anthony panicked when they saw my condition. They rushed me to hospital, where Doctor Bailey had his rooms. After examining me, he found that I had developed thrombosis.

He instructed the nurse to reserve a bed in the ward for further observation. He explained that blood clots in the leg were a serious condition and that, if a piece of the clot reached my lungs, it could be fatal.

I cried bitterly as they wheeled me to the ward where they treated me. Colleen cried when she heard that I was to be hospitalized once more. Megan made every effort to keep Colleen calm. The thought of being back in hospital made me troubled, as my old fears that I'd shoved deep down inside me started resurfacing. I was prepared for the worst but still prayed for the best. I'd developed a fear of the hospital.

The nurse on duty settled me into my room; my vital signs were observed. Abigail was surprised to see me and gave me special care again. She showed extra compassion for my setback.

Dr Bailey worked closely with the other caregivers while I was hospitalised. He prescribed medication that was to be injected at the same time every day to prevent further blood clots. He also prescribed support stockings that I had to wear every day.

As I lay in bed that night, crazy thoughts obsessed me, leaving me with little hope, as I remembered that my life was just a breath. The conflict within me made me question my strength. I wept for a long time, fearing that depression may set in. I was here for a purpose. I remembered when things were such a mess, I'd thought that recovery was unattainable. But I had fought and learnt that nothing was impossible.

I stayed a full week in hospital and then was discharged and given further treatment to administer at home.

When I got back home, my life became more complicated. I started my day at the physiotherapist and then rushed home to wait for the nurse to tend to the cleaning of my leg. In between, I went to the laboratory for regular blood tests to make sure that the correct amount of medication was administered to me to prevent further clots, as the wrong dosage could have damaging effects.

It was important that every appointment for my blood tests was kept, in order to adjust my medication according to the results. A booklet was handed to me to record all my blood readings on a weekly basis. I was also put on a special diet.

By now, I was comfortable using the crutches, and as a result, I moved about with no difficulty.

Almost four months went by since I was discharged from hospital; they were four very difficult months, but still, I got through each day. It seemed that the months had flown by, and my spirits were lifted. I began to walk farther distances, sometimes without my crutches, although very unsteadily. The testing continued until my blood was regular again. I was happy that my blood settled, and my visits to the clinic stopped. My hope was renewed once more when the testing came to an end.

In the interim, Renaldo advised me to appoint an attorney to register my accident with the Motor Insurance Fund. The process may be lengthy, but the money could possibly help to pay for my future medical expenses. It would also compensate me for any losses that were a result of the accident. The lawyer appointed to handle my case was confident that she could get the best results for me. She kept me updated and gave me a general overview of my case whenever it was necessary.

It was a pleasant surprise when Ann spent a Sunday afternoon with me. Her presence made a difference, as it took the boredom out of my day. I was very sensitive during the visit, but I managed to remain composed as I prepared myself emotionally for the friends I knew may pop in. I was excited to see her. We discussed my progress, and our closeness enabled me to share all my experiences of the past few months. She reminded me that I had my life to be thankful for and emphasised that, no matter how unfavourable my life was, someone, somewhere was fighting to be alive. My anxiety melted away. She was a source of positive energy for my state of mind and encouraged me to engage in physical activities and to meditate — two things she was good at.

I was fit enough to return to my workplace to personally monitor daily events. I worked on getting the business back on track, as things had gone wrong while I was away. I had to focus on the actions necessary to remedy the situation. I could not sit for long periods at a time. Therefore, I spent a few hours a day at work, although in general, I mastered more exercises and was getting sturdier by the day.

By now, I was also able to prepare meals for my family. My progress and the speed at which my healing took place had been nothing short of a blessing. I was a couple of months ahead of the doctors' predictions. By the sixth month, I was able to lose my crutches completely and walk freely. My soul was overflowing with confidence.

I stood outside in the warm sun for a long time, letting the picture of healing soak into my mind. The warmth of the wind caressed my skin as I straightened my body. My hands were free at last. I closed my eyes and pictured myself running along the riverside enjoying the sight of the greenery beside the waters. All I wanted to do was walk and walk. No more crutches and walking sticks. It was my family's prayers that had sustained me. I was blessed to have such wonderful people in my circle.

No one could possibly know what a near brush with death was like unless they lived through it themselves. It was a frightening experience that I hoped never to repeat. I spent almost three months in two different hospitals and was appreciative of what God had done in my life. It was time to embrace my healing. Getting back into the game was going to be a long-term struggle, which I was prepared to grab with both hands.

I became nervous when Anthony's family invited us to go out for dinner. Mixed emotions welled up in me about the idea of being seen in public on this social level. I had an 'oh-no' moment that flashed before me. Staying home felt safe and turned out to be my coping mechanism. I was reluctant, as the skin on my leg was still in the healing process. I was not yet free from the anxiety of being in a crowd of people.

I really did not want to go, but eventually made a conscious choice to accompany them and planned to enjoy myself. I would make sure to put an extra layer of bandages on my leg to avoid any seepage of fluid, additionally to minimise the risk of infection.

The time for being concealed and cowering in a corner in fear was over. I was no longer going to avoid people and friends. I didn't want to waste another minute being afraid; it was time to venture out.

Dinner was pleasant. I found myself socialising easily. After dinner, I joined the ladies as they chose to gamble while the guys sat in the bar having a few drinks. At one stage, I glanced at my cell phone. I panicked when I noticed that I'd missed a few calls from Colleen. I looked at the time; it was past midnight.

The noise of the gambling machines was deafening and had drowned out the sound of my cell phone. I was concerned because it was so late, and Colleen was normally asleep at this time. A dreadful feeling engulfed me. I phoned back. The news was worse than I could ever have expected.

I learnt that her boyfriend Ric had hung himself and died instantly. I was gasping for air. We were all devastated, as her baby, Kiara, was only seven months old.

We rushed back home to be with Colleen and give her the support she needed. When she saw us, she rushed to my side, sobbing bitterly. Her face was swollen from crying, and her eyes were bloodshot.

'Maybe you did not hear correctly; he could still be alive. Let us wait for confirmation before we assume the worst,' I whispered. All we could do was pray, but deep down, we had to face the reality that he was gone, as it was unlikely that such information would be wrongly conveyed.

We awoke early the next morning to offer our condolences to the family, but when they saw us, they did not allow us through the door. We could not understand why they would forbid us to enter their home. The moment was full of confusion as we looked at each other, hoping for answers. The questions flew around in my head. All we wanted to do was sympathise with the family; unfortunately, we were not permitted near them. What had we done that was so bad that we could not enter into their home?

Ric's father approached us, saying that Colleen had upset their son in the week, as they'd had an argument. He went on to say that Colleen had kept Kiara away from her father, and that was the reason he had taken his life. This statement did not make sense, as Ric had spent the previous day with Kiara. He'd even made a video of them spending time playing together. What a terrible accusation to make without having any evidence to back up their statement and actions!

The colour drained from my face as the shock of his words hit me. Everybody at the house turned around and stared at us with such contempt that I did not know where to put myself. I became very uncomfortable. At that moment, the spotlight effect made the world become small as I put my head down, hoping to avoid those who witnessed the incident. I wanted to shrink into the nearest hole. We immediately turned around and left their home, feeling shattered by their reproach.

The whole incident was so unexpected for my daughter. I had no idea how to comfort her. My heart was deeply anguished at these unpredicted accusations. I would have never anticipated that such events would be playing out before me.

We discovered the venue of where the ceremony was scheduled to take place. To be absent from the funeral was not good etiquette from our side. We agreed to attend the funeral together with some family and friends who accompanied us. We would have to see how the day progresses for us.

During the service, we sat at the back of the church, in the hope that no one would notice us. I fought back the tears of anguish as I wondered how such a tragedy could befall my daughter at the tender age of twenty-two.

Despite the family's objections, we remained stubborn as we proceeded to the cemetery. Once again, we stayed in the background where no one easily detected us. Our aim was to support Colleen through her grief. I was concerned what this might do to her. I desperately wanted her to be okay. She needed closure so that the past wouldn't haunt her future.

I recalled Colleen telling me that Ric was a very unhappy man. He'd threatened on numerous occasions that he was going to take his life, but I did not know that he was serious. If only I had listened and done something about it. It was a terrible time in our lives as we struggled with what could have possibly driven him to the point of taking his life. His death affected us, as our lives were entwined, and we'd spent many days in his company; we'd even gone on many holidays together.

I hoped that Colleen did not have feelings of guilt or believe she could have prevented his death from happening. Feelings of anger and abandonment would follow, but with the help of counselling she was sure to overcome part of her grieving. In the days that followed, Colleen was very emotional. She always looked sad. I speculated that she was reliving that horrible day. She found it difficult to accept all that had happened but also had to remain brave, especially for Kiara's sake. It was all right for her to cry, I told her.

Unfortunately, we will never know the answers as to why Ric did something so selfish as to leave a baby girl behind; things are seldom what they seem. It was sad to lose someone at such a young age with so many opportunities spread before him. Even though Colleen was at a very frail place in her life, with time, I believe she will be able to overcome the terrible allegations that had been thrown at her. It was difficult going to the stores because on numerous occasions people would stare at us and some of them even refused to serve us when we got to the pay point.

She was the victim of blame, and unnecessary pain was inflicted upon her. I could only imagine the grief she had to wrestle and live with. If only I could change this horrible time in her life that was tearing her apart. The past few days were awful, but I was certain that she would pick up the pieces and move on eventually.

10

It was time to unplug myself from the pressure I was going through, and enjoy a small holiday break. It was time to self soothe, and there was no better way to do that than to spend some time at the beach and move away from the experiences of the past few days by putting them behind me. It was the perfect time to de-stress and have a dose of sun. We could spend uninterrupted time together. Maybe this would cheer us up and melt away some of our problems.

'How about another small vacation; maybe we can go to the beach and spend some time together?' I insisted to Anthony on his weekend visit home.

The last holiday we had taken together was before my accident. That weekend had turned out to be a disaster, with us arguing the whole time. He showed anger to everyone throughout the holiday by snapping at the waiters in the restaurant for no apparent reason.

I tried to block out his previous behaviour and continued to make the arrangements for a small break. I was hoping that this trip would turn out differently. This would be a good opportunity for us to reconnect. I was feeling very pleased with the idea, but he seemed uninterested. I ignored his attitude and went ahead with my plans. I found suitable accommodation.

'Maybe we could work on our marriage. Who knows? This break might do us the world of good.' I smiled encouragingly at him.

He just nodded in agreement.

Filled with anticipation, I began to pack for our weekend vacation. I was hopeful that the time we spent together on holiday could possibly bridge the gap that developed between us, and we might grow close again. It was not easy to admit that things were not going well in our marriage, but for now I wanted to get our relationship back on track, as well as to engage in working through the major issues that were weighing our marriage down.

We set out on our journey in the early hours of Friday morning. The weather was cool, with an early morning mist in the air. The drive was tedious, as we hardly uttered a word to each other. I attempted on numerous occasions to make conversation, but every time I was met with one-word answers. The silence between us was smothering.

At the halfway stop, he spent the entire time on his phone, avoiding contact with me, pretending that I did not exist.

'Who are you speaking to?' I asked him curiously.

'It's work related,' he mumbled under his breath.

I didn't believe him. We continued the journey in silence. *Why do I feel like I wasted my time taking this trip? Why did I even think that this holiday would be different from the other vacations we embarked on?* I wondered regretfully.

A couple of hours later, we reached our holiday venue, and then I began to unpack. Once again, he was glued to his phone. As hard as I tried to overlook our situation, it was impossible to disregard.

'Look, I did not come all this way to watch you spend the entire time on your phone. If this is the way it's going to be, we might as well pack up and go back home,' I snapped at him furiously.

He just gave me an indifferent look and pocketed his phone. By now, my heart was pounding with anger. I watched as all the planning, together with the money spent for the vacation, went up in smoke. No sooner than we arrived at what was supposed to be a happy event, I instead wanted to go back home.

I perceived this trip to be an obligation to him, rather than a chance for us to spend quality time together, as it was obvious that we were not alone. Our meals were taken in silence. His best friend was his phone. He spent hours texting her while I was lying next to him in bed. Everything we did together seemed to be a painful effort for him. He struggled to put on an act of happiness.

Most of the vacation was spent either arguing with or ignoring each other. Our walk on the beach was a disaster, with me walking slightly ahead of him. The escapade turned out to be a waste of time. I desperately wanted to get away from him to find time to clear my mind. The effort I made to try and salvage our marriage was not agreed to in good faith on his side.

The only conclusion I could draw from here was that our marriage was over. It was so easy to miss the obvious. I was striving for something that no longer existed. The love was gone. He was in love, but clearly it was not with me. There was a third party in our relationship that was tearing me down. It was me against them. His actions revealed his intentions with this other woman, and she was always in the wings of our marriage, like a shadow that refused to go away. The love we'd once shared disappeared without the possibility of revival. I was more upset than I let on.

It was time to face the hard truth and stop deceiving myself by pretending all was normal. I was not prepared to be a second choice for anyone.

I was relieved that we were going home the next day. I'd had enough of hiding from the truth. I was fooling myself and came to the conclusion that I was no longer happy. We achieved absolutely nothing by being together; instead, the holiday took an ominous turn. Failure weighed heavily on my shoulders. I don't know which felt worse — failure of the marriage or my loss of self-respect for pursuing the marriage. A distance grew between us that threw us a million miles apart. I was very happy when we reached home.

I started to unpack at once. I kept a smile on my face, in the hope that the children would not detect that anything was amiss, as I knew they might soak up the discomfort and become insecure.

I undressed, showered, and lay awake staring at the ceiling for hours. This seemed to be the role I played every night. The ceiling seemed to be my big flat screen. My body was exhausted due to lack of sleep. I began taking sleeping tablets just to get some rest.

No more! I thought to myself. My day of reckoning had come. It was my moment to get to the bottom of the problem. I made my choice to address our situation with Anthony. He gave me a cynical look, insisting that he did not notice anything different in our marriage. Nothing had changed as far as he was concerned. He sounded like an accomplished liar, looking at me straight in the face, challenging my loyalty.

I was outraged by his response and looked at him in disbelief. It was hopeless to pursue the topic further or ask any more questions because he would deny the matter anyway. I'm not sure how he viewed our situation as being okay or even that nothing changed.

He created his own world of fantasy. I was on the outside. Once fooled was more than enough for me, but twice fooled was definitely a shame on me. I was done with pretending that our marriage was on track, because it was not. I was fired up. It was time to stand up for myself, time to snoop around his possessions and get out of this mess and find out the truth.

While he was taking a shower, I took the opportunity of browsing through his phone. My heart was pumping, and my hands were clammy as I began to glance through his messages. There it was, all the evidence staring at me in the face. His infidelity hovered over me like a thunderstorm. There were messages from a woman named Avril; her messages revealed how much she loved him. There were lots of pictures of hearts and kisses attached. As I saw a picture of the way she dressed, I thought back to the gypsy's words—'a person who does not eat the same kind of food as you'.

This can't be happening. Was she of Muslim religion? Was she the lady who was a threat to my marriage?

I could not tell for certain. There were also messages from a woman by the name of Ronel. Her messages portrayed that he lived with her while he was working on-site. I must have had an astounded expression on my face as I continued reading his messages that revealed that she was desperately trying to hang onto him while he had lost interest in her.

As I continued to browse through his phone messages, I got the impression that Avril was his latest lover, and they were very serious about each other. After much deliberation, I concluded that he was the type who quickly lost interest and moved on to the next one. It all started making sense. This explained all those disappearances, going to the car wash and coming back with an unclean car, and the excuses of all the late nights at work. It also explained why he could not take my phone calls. Instead, he chose to call me back when he was not in her company.

Despite having the evidence before me, I was uncomfortable. I wanted a confession. There was a sudden alarm vibrating within me. *How could I have been so blind when it was in front of me all along, staring at me?* I was uncertain how to address his unfaithfulness. I thought long and hard about how to resolve this painful situation.

I assumed there was only one way of doing it — that is, to tell him that it was over. Whichever way it turned out, I would try my best to be emotionless for the sake of my sanity. I'd held back for as long as I could. It was time to be true to myself.

'Who is Avril?' I asked, as soon as he stepped out of the bath.

'I have no idea,' he replied uneasily.

His response startled me. 'I have been through your phone, and I have read all the messages you exchanged with her and Ronel. How can you deny it when the facts are before us?'

He'd crossed the cheating line and was in denial. He looked like a trapped animal standing some distance away, with his head down, not daring to raise his eyes as I continued to question him. He remained silent throughout my questioning. I'm not sure whether he was shocked at being caught out or angry that I had gone through his phone.

He became aggressive and began to scream at me. He eventually flung his phone against the wall. He was furious that I'd skimmed through his phone and said very hurtful things. I should have guessed that the confrontation would be met with denial and aggression, but I was not about to back down, as I'd seen the facts for myself.

'You have no right to go through my phone. I need my privacy!' He could not keep his temper under control.

'There shouldn't *be* any privacy between us!' I responded as I regained my composure.

We stared at each other awkwardly. Our marriage seemed to have boundaries—you stay on your side while I stay on mine.

Without saying a word, he marched up and down in the room while admitting to his affairs. He was cornered and confessed very sorrowfully. I managed to mine the facts from him, even though he was not completely honest and tried his best to bend the truth to make himself look better, ultimately getting himself out of the difficult situation of being caught.

'I have been seeing her for almost five years. It started as a casual fling. I did not think that it was going to last this long.' It sounded like a cheap, ridiculous joke.

'Wow … five years. Clearly it never stopped. Was it worth it?' I paused as I waited for a response.

None came.

'Out of curiosity, why did you do it? Never mind, don't answer me on any of the questions I have asked. It does not matter anymore.' I smiled falsely and became even tenser thinking of these two women and wondering how many others there were.

'There is no future for us.' My words were a whisper but also a promise to myself, as I needed to consider what was important for me. It was time to stand up for myself in a firm way, as I was the keeper of my own happiness. I was not about to surrender to his games. I was emotionally compromised, and that did not sit well with me.

'On second thoughts and as a matter of interest, I *would* like you to answer my question. Where were you meeting her?' I insisted.

'In restaurants, hotels; I would take her out to dinner. But she means nothing to me. I am not in love with her. She is just an infatuation.'

I was bruised at the confession and the cover-up lies. He was deluded if he thought I bought any of his betrayal. When was the last time I was taken out to a restaurant, let alone to a hotel?

'Don't go there; it is so wrong. Infatuation does not last for five years!' I snapped at him. At the same time, I had the urge to strangle him.

It was obvious that our marriage had disintegrated. I did not know how to fix it or even that I wanted to fix it. No one had ever made me feel so low in my life. He made me feel worthless. I should have checked it out immediately when I had my suspicions.

I was beyond hurt; I almost felt ashamed that I did not act on the warning signs before now. Even though I'd had my suspicions, I'd failed to accept them.

I moved into the spare room. His deception was unsettling. There was very little left to salvage. The affairs explained the miserable failing of our marriage.

There was no way that I could stay in a hurtful marriage that made me feel that I deserved no better. It all became complicated, with very little indication of what the solution would be. Looking at the magnitude of my problem, I was forced to reconsider everything about my life and confront the actuality, as he was not prepared to own up to his mistakes.

I would never recover the time that had passed; nor would I trust him again. Every recollection of the day would haunt me for a long time to come. I was wakeful and tossed and turned for what seemed like hours.

We hardly spoke to each other in the days that followed. When we did have a discussion, he kept pleading for forgiveness, making false promises to make it right and assuring me that it wouldn't happen again. I avoided him and concentrated on my business, which kept me occupied full-time.

Nobody was to blame for where I was sitting but myself. Although I kept blaming myself, I also knew that, at this point, it did not matter whose fault it was; the deed was done. Frightening thoughts of revenge started going through my mind. There was no future for us. It was time let it go and protect what was left of my reputation.

I woke up weary from lack of sleep, then watched the sun rise every morning. My mind was disturbed with images of them together. How could I pretend and continue living a lie? How could I allow him to touch me? The wall between us became impenetrable; it was too high to climb. My world was coming to an end. How could I forgive? Would I ever be able to forgive him and continue with my life as if this has never happened? A strong feeling of hostility overtook me, but I would ride the waves of the numbness I was feeling.

The weekend was over, and I was relieved that it was time for him to go back to work. It was a good thing that he was still working away from home. It gave me time to deal with our problems.

He'd stopped providing me with funds to support the family along with the running costs of the house ages ago.

Every month, his income took care of his needs. When I did ask for financial assistance, he refused outright and became defensive. I was taking care of all household and personal expenses to keep the family together — from college fees to the basic needs of my family — making sure that bills were paid and the kids were fed and seeing to all the essentials.

I needed to put a distance between us and make a clean break. It was time for me to get the wheels in motion. The ideal platform was set. On his next weekend home, I would inform him about my decision for a divorce. It was a scary decision, but I had to take the risk, irrespective of whatever repercussions might arise from my actions. I wanted more out of my life. This was not it. My age made things a bit more complex, but staying in an unhappy marriage could have terrible emotional effects on me and the children.

It was a Friday evening when he arrived home. I waited for him to settle down before approaching the subject. The tough moment arrived. Hoping for a civil dialogue between us, I plucked up the courage to inform him that I could not spend the rest of my life with someone who did not respect me. In a flash, Anthony packed his belongings, departing with the screeching of wheels. My three daughters were shattered. They could not accept what was transpiring, even though they knew about the anguish I was going through. I assumed that they may well be angry about my decision, but I prepared myself for their reactions.

'No one should have to go through this. What will people say about us?' they protested. They mumbled to each other but were indirectly addressing me. The blame all shifted onto me! He was exonerated from all blame for the failed marriage.

It made my heart ache to think I appeared to be the bad person. Colleen and Robyn also left the house in tears. I assumed that they were trying to digest the news that they received.

They returned later that evening and went straight to their bedrooms. My feelings would have to be put aside to give my marriage another chance and then deal with the breach of trust. I'd planned this through, but it was not going the way I thought it should. Further dishonour was on my plate, as I had to back out of my plans because my children objected to my intentions and made it apparent. I was not the one having the affairs. *He* was the one and was doing a great job at it. Now I understood how love could turn to hate and, why so many people remained in dead, loveless marriages while people on the outside were so quick to judge. My mind was foggy, doubting that perfect relationships existed.

He returned home later that evening after pleading calls from his children.

I made sure that I remained in my room, pretending to be asleep to avoid any confrontation. I was engulfed in a feeling of emptiness as I stared morosely in front of me. I was so outraged for having to stay in a loveless marriage.

I switched on the television, thinking that, if I watched the late-night news, my mind would be distracted. To my horror, the first hospital where I was treated appeared on the screen. My mouth fell open as I watched the news with disbelief. The hospital was being accused of harvesting body parts! I had a flashback to my nightmares. All my senses were alert. I had a tightening feeling in my stomach as I searched my body to check for signs of any missing organs—not that I would find them missing by searching or feeling my body.

The following morning, I made a dash for the phone to make an appointment with my doctor to confirm that all my body parts were intact. I was sure that they would have picked it up in the time I lay in the hospital. I insisted on a physical check-up to put my mind at ease.

To my relief, when the doctors checked, all my organs were intact; none were missing.

Once again, my mind went back to the conversations I'd thought I heard when I was in a coma. Maybe there *was* some truth to several of the incidents and they weren't just hallucinations!

Something about the hospital was unclear, but I could not put my finger on it. Certain events in my nightmares I'd had while in a coma were unfolding now; it petrified me. The nightmares were starting to blend with real things that were happening to me.

Later that day, I did my own research into the hospital. I discovered information that was scandalous. There were terrible reports from displeased patients who'd lost family members due to negligence. There was also an article about a young girl who discovered that her kidney was missing. It was frightening. The hospital was under the scanner for doing shameful deeds. *Had I almost been a victim of organ harvesting?*

11

I stared at my phone for a good few seconds. I became uneasy as I noticed that I'd missed a call from Anthony while I was in church on Sunday morning. As I reached my front door, he called again. I attempted to remain calm, as he never called that early on a Sunday but usually called late in the afternoon. I did not want to think of the worst as I answered his next call.

He explained that he was on his way to do some shopping. When I ended the call, I thought that was strange information to share. He could have just gone to buy the items that he needed. He called again a while later, telling me about the chest pains he was experiencing. I realized then, that when he'd placed the call earlier, he must have already not been feeling well, which was why he really called in the first place, and not to tell me where he was going. He most probably did not want me to be alarmed.

'I have chest pains. I am driving myself to the nearest hospital.'

There was a tightness in my stomach as he spoke. I panicked because I was aware of his health conditions.

I phoned regularly throughout the day, worried that chest pains could be associated with a heart attack. When he reached the hospital, he called again to update me that he would be staying overnight at the hospital so that the doctors could monitor his chest pains.

The following morning, I received another call from a nurse stating that a helicopter was about to airlift him to a hospital that specialised in cardiology. The word 'helicopter' sent all sorts of warning signals running through my mind. For a minute, my world seemed to stand still. I began to feel guilty because of our fight on his last visit, but I brushed my thoughts aside in an effort to process whatever it was that I needed to deal with.

I received another call from a senior doctor, bringing me up to date on his condition and verifying that it was necessary to perform a triple bypass. He explained that Anthony had a blocked artery, which is a serious condition whereby the heart was not pumping enough blood to other parts of his body. The doctors were afraid that the clots they'd found might dislodge themselves and endanger his life further.

I closed my eyes for a minute, absorbing the information I'd received. I held my breath, imagining certain disasters that could befall him. I whispered a silent prayer for his healing and petitioned for strength to face what lay ahead. The doctor's words caused my adrenaline to soar, leaving a dryness in my mouth. My mind began to race to the worst-case scenario. I immediately began to make arrangements to be at his side, asking Shaun to accompany me.

We began our journey the following day. The skies were cloudy, and the rain was pelting down. The foggy weather brought about a feeling of bleakness. The trip was eventful, with many stops because of the heavy rainfall. Contrary to our mood, the atmosphere was filled with a fresh smell of the earth from the rain as we travelled to our destination. We booked into a nearby hotel.

On arrival we discovered that the operation was scheduled for that afternoon. We were allowed a brief visit with him. We assured him that the operation would be a success.

We returned six hours later, to be informed by the nurse on duty that his triple bypass operation was successful. She allowed us to see him for a short time, as he was still asleep. He looked at peace as we stood at his bedside.

Anthony's family arrived on Saturday to spend the day with him, and they all returned home that same day, while Shaun and I remained behind. I spent as much time as possible at his bedside.

On further examinations, the doctors discovered that his diabetes was not controlled. It had progressed to another stage. He was not responding to the current treatment. His treatment plan had to change to keep his blood sugar levels within a healthy range. His medication was replaced with insulin injections. The doctor warned him that, if it was not treated, it could lead to major complications, such as a stroke, kidney disease, or even another heart attack.

He was disturbed by the diagnosis of his diabetes. The thought that he would be required to take the injection for the rest of his life was difficult for him to accept. He considered that this new finding might disrupt his quality of life.

A meeting between Anthony, the dietician, and myself was held to brief us on the way forward regarding his diet and physical activity. The dietician explained that, being a diabetic patient, Anthony needed to be aware that maintaining a good blood glucose level was the solution to dealing with his condition. She continued to inform us that he needed to change his daily habits by adjusting his lifestyle. He was compelled to take his insulin daily before his meals. He also needed to check his blood sugar levels often.

The medical team gave him booklets with instructions on how to take care of his health. My mind wandered as she was explaining the dos and don'ts.

Will I be able to enjoy my life with all these restrictions to my diet?' Anthony whispered. He was feeling vulnerable.

I consoled him that it would work out well as long as he followed the doctor's instructions. It was essential for him to control his sugar intake, as he enjoyed sweet things and overindulged in the wrong foods.

He spent an additional four days in hospital. The next day, he was discharged, and then we headed home. The four-hour journey was miserable. He was in a terrible frame of mind throughout the trip. He became depressed.

On the second day at home, he informed me that he'd arranged a meeting with his manager. I was confused, as the doctor had given him strict instructions that he was not to exert himself, let alone drive. According to the doctor's advice, recovery from a heart bypass could take up to twelve weeks for the breastbone to heal. He also recommended that, during the healing process, Anthony was to avoid physical activity and was not to do anything strenuous, like lifting heavy objects. He was not to drive until advised by his doctor.

He insisted that he was attending a meeting, which was work related and urgent. I knew deep in my heart that this was one of his excuses to get away; it was not his manager that he was meeting. He took great care with his appearance. He was clearly going to meet his girlfriend, Avril. Seriously! He just had a triple bypass, and two days later, he was behind the wheel. It was insane. Did he not care about his health?

My heart was broken as I watched him get into his car and watched as it vanished down the road. This continued throughout the month while he was supposedly recovering.

He returned to work without having the rest that the doctor prescribed for him.

Fortunately for him, his manager allowed him to work nearer home while he was healing. When he was fully recovered, he was expected to return to the construction site.

I questioned my faith as I looked back to all the tender nursing I'd provided for him over the past month. He could no longer hide or even pretend anymore; his actions were obvious to me. Where was his sense of right and wrong?

The ground had been shaken from under my feet. I started to wonder how many infidelities there were in the past. How would I respect him after his selfish actions? An apology would not make it right this time. I could not look the other way anymore, hoping that the affairs would pass. I made every effort to stop myself from obsessing over the details but, rather, come to terms with why this awful incident was happening to me. My plan of action needed to be determined.

My heart was heavy as I took a closer look at my negative situation. I judged my life to be unfair. I needed courage to do the right thing, to separate myself from the people and issues that were making me unhappy. For now, Anthony was pulling me down.

12

To improve my life, I plucked up the courage to drive further distances. I was confident enough to return to work full-time. The phobia of getting into the driver's seat after my accident had left me completely. I was thrilled by the fact that I was driving again.

I loved the freedom and the independence of jumping into my car and freely getting from one point to another. I immediately set upon a plan of action to turn the business around to become profitable. The business had gone through a particularly stressful patch over the past few months, as nothing was as I'd left it before my accident.

Working for a few hours a day did not improve the situation. My business required my full attention. It was my priority to get the solutions for the business to proceed smoothly to the next level. There were glitches that I faced. Putting all the pieces together to figure out what had taken place during my absence kept me busy. I pushed through the struggles and watched as my business made a comeback.

My confidence returned. I loved every bit of the challenges that I faced. The game was different to the corporate world where I spent most of my working career. I looked forward to the days ahead and accepted the accomplishments, as well as the hardships that cropped up. I loved the excitement of the daily trends in the market, where comparisons were made to measure market-related information pertaining to pricing of merchandise.

The enlisting of new clients took up most of my time. It involved countless phone calls and sourcing information from friends and social media platforms, which kept me busy throughout the day. The many meetings and setting up appointments also demanded my full attention.

With these daily aspects of the business, my mind had no time to meditate on undesirable thoughts. I received compliments from many people, who commented on the impressive way that I pulled it back from the spiral and the strategies I put into place for its improvement.

'It took a lot of hard work and commitment to arrive at this point,' was my modest response.

I was satisfied by the outcome, regardless of the work that still lay ahead to enhance our practices. We were on the path of revival, and that was enough for now. It was good to be back in the game. From the profit that we generated, we managed to upgrade some of our equipment. I was proud of my ability to overcome the obstacles as I did. I learnt to follow my dreams and to have self-belief, which was very important to me.

In the meantime, my case with the fund was still ongoing. Four years passed. There was still no progress. The solicitor appointed to my case requested for me to consult with their medical experts to assess my injuries for them to compile a report for my compensation claim. The purpose of the consultations was to establish the impact the injuries had on my job function and my daily life. Arrangements were made for pictures to be taken of all my visible scarring and bruising. The process seemed tiring, just thinking about the requirements. During one of my examinations, a doctor left me half-dressed in a passage as people walked to and from the other adjoining consulting rooms. I found this to be extremely unprofessional.

On another occasion, I was seated in a very confined space completing questionnaires while the doctor's assistant, who was supposed to assist me, locked himself up in a room with a woman friend who appeared in the middle of my appointment. I called out to him several times, but he blatantly ignored me. I eventually banged on the door to let him know that I completed the forms.

As he opened his door, he was still in the process of pulling up his pants. I have never, in my entire life, experienced such unethical manners in the medical field!

In addition, further information, together with more supporting documents, were required from my lawyer with regard to my business activities. The auditor who was appointed from the opposing side continued to request information that I'd already supplied several times. This was inherently cumbersome and costly.

My claim could not be settled through negotiation and, therefore, was escalated to the high court on two occasions. On both counts, the court was unable to come up with a settlement figure. Strangely, it was difficult for them to reach a decision from the many comprehensive tests, examinations, and discussions that were held to determine and quantify the compensation due to me.

I did whatever was required from my side, as I reminded myself that the incentive to persevere was that it would pay off in the end.

Unexpectedly, Anthony became unsettled at his workplace.

He was frustrated and, threatening to leave his employment to join me in the running of my business. He complained about the reshuffling of the employees at his workplace; in addition, his manager was planning to increase his workload. His company also planned to move him into a smaller lodge to cut down on costs.

On inspection of the new lodge allocated to him, he discovered that it was poorly ventilated. He also found dampness in the walls. He was dissatisfied with these changes, as they affected his health negatively.

After giving it a great deal of thought, I advised him that it was not a wise decision for him to leave his job at this point to join me, as the business was just starting to become financially stable. It was risky for both of us to be working in one place. But at the same time, I was obliged to consider his health.

His phone calls asking to join me became more desperate; he pleaded to return home. I suggested he look for employment first before joining me, but I also advised him to do what he thought was best for his health. I did not want to be held accountable for the repercussions of his actions, in case it did not work out in his favour by me making the final decision.

Having him on board might be feasible, as he could possibly assist Colleen in managing the business during the times I attended to other pressing matters, but those concerns were unlikely to last forever. He proceeded to give notice to his company.

After a month he joined Colleen and myself in the business. The timing at this point was overlapping with my plans, in the sense that the business was not functioning like before but was progressing at a steady pace. He insisted on being paid an unreasonable salary, which the company could not afford. He claimed that he needed to pay his bills, which was strange, as I was paying all the bills in the house. Furthermore, there was a distance in our relationship that I was still trying to deal with. The thought of having him around day and night felt stifling.

Even though it was a challenge to maintain a balance between work and home, we worked through our reservations. At the beginning, there were no issues, as we started to learn from one another. It was not always easy to relax and leave the day's events at the office. Some days, working together had its benefits, as the responsibilities were shared. We tried to refrain from discussing work-related issues at home, but on the odd occasion, we remained in the work mode, discussing urgent matters.

With our positive attitude, all went smoothly. We remained focused on our clients and business strategies. We continuously embraced the daily challenges by responding to them with keenness. I assumed that our success was guaranteed.

In spite of all the effort and hard work I put into the business, Anthony suddenly disapproved of my decision-making and hindered the management of the business. I gathered that it was a lousy idea for us to be working together. Not even a year had passed when we began to have heated differences of opinion about the outcome we visualised for the company. Keeping our personal feelings separate from work became impossible, as we could not agree on anything. It became awkward to steer back and forth between our private life and our professional one.

The system started to fall apart, as he adamantly overrode my instructions. He took over my management duties while imposing his own rules. The business objectives became disrupted, as he constantly opposed the practices of the business that were put in place and that worked. The customers gave me negative feedback, complaining about the shortage of stock. Anthony ignored the procurement process, which enabled the company to accurately record goods and services from external suppliers. The business was compromised by these changes and exposed to theft.

I received a call from one of my clients, who informed me that Anthony was continuously on his phone during delivery time. They were unable to enquire about the stock they were receiving. He was not managing the delivery procedures and took shortcuts by signing the book without checking any of the goods.

I was disappointed that he so inconsiderately put the company in jeopardy. The staff became insecure, as our differences of opinion became more evident and affected the team. Pat walked into my office one morning to enquire how much longer Anthony would be working at the company. She also stated that the employees were afraid of him, as he made discriminatory remarks to them.

'If these remarks continue, I don't see the staff being loyal to you,' she told me. 'They have been in discussions about giving you notice or walking out if he continues to disrespect them. Everyone in the office is on edge. We are forced to walk around on eggshells when he is around.'

I promised to investigate their grievances and address their issues with him in an effort to resolve the complaints. The dissatisfaction that the employees were experiencing became apparent and could be seen in their lack of interest and likewise in their low productivity. Avoiding this situation may prove unfavourable to the company.

I approached him about the missing stock, along with the complaints from the employees, but he shrugged it off with a denial, claiming that nothing of the sort was taking place. He insisted that he checked all items of stock accordingly.

'How do you explain the missing stock, which amounts to such a huge sum of money?' I demanded.

He could not account for his action; instead, he looked at me as though I was the one that didn't know what I was talking about.

The business began to sink gradually because of all the unexplained disappearance of stock, combined with the mismanagement.

To crown it all, there was a fraud case in the company that was ongoing, and the authorities were unable to resolve the case.

The total sum of money lost was the same amount that appeared in my dream while I was disorientated and abducted by three men on a train in hospital. How were the two linked? Why the coincidence of the amount? I struggled to understand the bigger picture, but to no avail; instead, I got a sinking feeling that left me feeling very discouraged.

As if these burdens were not bad enough, I received an unexpected phone call from one of my major clients telling me to respond to an email they sent to me. My heartbeat quickened at his abrupt tone of voice, as I thought that we always provided a good service to him. I immediately opened my email.

The information unsettled me, as it pointed out the poor service the client was receiving from our company and the shortage of stock. It took my client a day to set up a meeting to discontinue our contract due to negligence and unprofessional performance on our part. I found myself speculating where in our service had we gone astray.

All I could do was to take stock of the damage. I lost my major client who had been with me for over five years. I later learned that Anthony had a run-in with one of the security staff at my client's workplace, which had almost resulted in a fistfight. There was no way out of this messy tight spot.

Staff members were put on short time. Expenses were paid from an income that was rapidly declining. To say the least, the whole business was in shutdown mode. I had no idea where to turn to or what to do. Whichever way we ventured, we reached a dead end. We could not find a solution to the endless calamities that kept popping up.

I'd never anticipated such a drastic change in my business venture. It was clear as I took a closer look that the change had not happened overnight. The business had begun to fail a while back. The signs were everywhere, specifically when the employees started becoming restless, but I had failed to take any action early enough to save the company because of my trust in Anthony. I could not blame circumstances or anybody else for that matter, as I should have done something about it a while ago. Instead, I'd avoided addressing the subject, hoping that it would miraculously repair itself or go away. I'd ignored the problems, pretending that they did not exist, but they became progressively worse as time went on. It was impossible for the business to subsist, as we'd used all the capital that had been reserved to fall back on.

To make matters even worse, Anthony was not prepared to look for another job but continued to sit around in the hope that production might miraculously transform for the better. It amazed me when he suggested that I should leave the business to him.

Furthermore, he persuaded me to look for other employment.

How dare he even think that was an option? I had spent ten hard years making my business a success, and he believed that he could just waltz in and take over! His face was buried in his computer or phone day in and day out. I watched him sitting idle, astonished at what he could achieve by doing nothing all day, let alone take over the business he was not even prepared to learn about. He still disappeared for hours on end always had flimsy excuses, which worsened the trust issues in our marriage.

As always, it was, 'I'm going to resolve my billing on the phone,' or, 'I'm going to look for car parts, as something is wrong with my car.' His brand-new car always seemed to have problems—the same brand-new car that he'd demanded I pay for in full. His excuses were endless. He acted in his own self- interest and did not realise that his lies were becoming destructive, because the trust between us was shrinking even more. His lies made up for other lies, not changing. Like any liar he would be exposed one day. I could not change his conduct, but I could change the way I reacted to it.

13

It was difficult to drag my thoughts away from my concerns. My opinions were wandering through random battles in my mind. I was not there in the moment. My mind was racing to so many things that could have been handled differently, careless decisions that could have been avoided. I was feeling overly miserable because of the change in my situation, which was difficult to disregard.

There was no break in the succession of hardships that I was going through. This was causing my trust in God to dwindle. By now, my level of faith was almost non-existent. The rental owed on our property was accumulating. The bank was phoning to demand the payment repeatedly. It was hard to sleep at night thinking about the figures my accountant tossed at me in regards to my business.

By this time, the company was heavily borrowed on, with huge debts that were still progressing. Two of my vehicles were sold to pay some of the debts in order to survive within our means. It was not easy. My pride was hurt more than anything else. I knew I had done an amazing job thus far, so I was really deflated when I became aware that it was the end. My hole was becoming deeper and darker. It was time to throw in the towel. The whole system was against me.

'Hannah, I suggest you move on from here. There is no sense in sitting around and having endless meetings hoping things will change on their own. Consider cutting your losses so that you don't wind up in worse financial trouble. You are running up your costs and accruing your bills,' Elise, my accountant, cautiously recommended during one of our meetings.

She had been examining my books for over a week. Of course, she was right because we'd watched as our debts had accumulated. There was no real proposal in place. We paid what was most urgent. A cloud of stress hung over me, as I lived in a constant state of heightened anxiety. The balance sheets and financial statements were all finalised.

Two weeks later, the temporary closing of the business was put into motion. The most frightening thing was to watch the business's doors bang shut. I was extremely sad to lose my business, but there was nothing I could do for now. These were the cold, hard facts.

Yet, I still had hope that my situation might change. The business was only temporarily closed. Despite all I was going through, I knew deep down in my heart that I would open my doors again, especially with all my knowledge and experience that I'd gained along the way. I reassured myself that this was not failure; it was just a slight interruption. It was very far from the end of the game for me.

I was feeling miserable with the way my life was turning out. I wanted to escape from the pain. Everything looked different, not at all what I'd envisioned. Regardless, I would overcome any resistance in my path for the reason that I still believed in myself.

We hired a truck to put all the machinery in storage. I had to find the courage to let go what I could not change for now. My memories took me back to the time when it was just Colleen and me in the business. I couldn't help but think of how motivated we were. There were no squabbles or disagreements; each day was fairly smooth. We worked hard every day, and the results were very rewarding.

The reality of my predicament had yet to sink in. This was another chapter in my life that had closed, but I consoled myself that every end had a new beginning. We all sat at home, hoping for some miracle to fall from the sky.

'Pray until something happens,' Robyn reminded me.

I thought long and hard about those words as well as the powerful impact they had on me. My mother had instilled in my belief in the power of prayer, and the faith to turn to prayer, especially when I was feeling down; it would certainly stay with me for life.

'I trust in you, God. Where did I go wrong?' I said aloud this particular morning when I awoke. 'I am faithful to you; I pray often. Why is this happening to me?'

I recalled a passage from my prayer book and recited the words whenever I felt dispirited:

I cling to you, Lord. I put my faith in you. I trust that all will go well because you have a plan in all this – even if the circumstances seem impossible. There will be good that will come out of these hard times. Please help me to keep my eyes fixed on you as you go before me today. Keep me close to you always. Please help me to keep doing what is right. Give me the strength to run my race till the end.

Now, I prayed these words over and over in my mind. God was not done with me yet. He did not bring me this far to leave me. I'd journeyed a long way and had made it thus far, not by chance, but by faith. God's presence was with me.

Life has pulled me in different directions, but I will continue my journey because something bigger than I imagined was still to come. This was only a temporary inconvenience. I held onto these declarations. I was given sorrow, which was painful. But every sentiment was worth it, as I got to know the unexpected reserve of the strength in me.

Life was full of twists and turns. The days turned into months. Still, no work was forthcoming. There were unending phone calls made and meetings that we attended, but still nothing. We were on the verge of losing our home to the bank, as we were behind with payment by a few months by now. Worry was the order of the day. I could not see past what I hoped for.

As I looked at Anthony, he seemed to have aged overnight and was filled with concern. I thought for a moment that, even though we had plenty of friends and relatives, there was not one name that came to light at this crucial time as far as someone who could possibly accommodate us or even help us financially.

Anthony turned to his two brothers for relief to take care of his bills and assist with some of the bills at home.

'What are we going to do?' I asked him one morning as he paced the room with his head down. The distant expression on his face told me that his mind was faraway.

'This is one time that I don't have any answers; we need to sell whatever we can to survive,' he said with a desperate smile.

My confidence left me, as I experienced true self-doubt. I was afraid of what others might say and think. I was afraid of failing. But I chose to be less worried by what people were thinking and to ignore any negative judgements. Everyone has lived through bad times at some stage of his or her life; I was just living through mine.

From there, the selling began. Some of my machinery from the business was vended. I was despondent as I watched each item being sold off, but I knew from my experiences of growing up that I would be able to replace each item at some point with more modern machines.

I convinced myself to remain positive, as I was not about to give up on my dreams. I continued to believe in myself. I would learn from the critical events that had led to where I was. I am no saint, and I have done a few wrong things in my life. I have questioned my abilities and my past and present decisions. But I also know I have done good things too. Knowing this has made me see that I can overcome my obstacles. I shouldn't have to compromise on my values or give in to this test. I understood that things in life are temporary; we enjoy them when it goes well and become pessimistic when it goes poorly. It was only natural for me to desire the best. Notwithstanding all this positive self-talk, I sat in my chair feeling tired. Anthony was drinking worse than ever. The drinking started early on the weekends and continued throughout the night till the end of the weekend. I dreaded weekends because of this.

Friends and family were in and out of my home, so they saw it all. I was starting to feel that my home was just a house, not a home anymore. I was at my wit's end with the drinking. The situation became tiring—loud music and talking that went on late into the night as though there was no tomorrow. The combination of what was happening in my home, including the problems I was dealing with, made me helpless. These were the facts I had to live with.

Anthony's brother Raven walked into my kitchen one Friday afternoon while I was preparing dinner, with his refreshments in his hand. He enquired as to how I was doing.

'Not so good,' I responded. 'I think my marriage is in trouble.'

It was a plea for help, but he stared at me with his lip curling slightly and shrugged his shoulders as if I had not uttered a word. I knew he'd heard every word I said, but he was not interested. My plea did not matter.

Why had he bothered to ask the question? I was left confused. I detected some tension as he walked back into the entertainment area where they always sat enjoying each other's company. I found myself scanning his attitude for problems, but I convinced myself that maybe he really had nothing to say.

When everyone went home and Anthony went to bed, I cleaned up after them so that I did not have to wake up to a messy house. This was my weekend routine. I could not sleep at night; all my worries kept popping into my mind. I was constantly on edge. My emotions would spin out of control, ranging from anger to hostility, leaving me feeling flat.

Sundays were difficult days for Anthony. He basically slept the whole day, trying to nurse his hangover, which seemed to have slowed him down. He was sensitive to everything around him, even the slightest noise.

It had been over a year since we started sleeping in separate bedrooms. It was on days like these that I was grateful to be in my own space for my mental health, hence putting me in a relaxed state that was conducive to my quality of sleep and free of all unwanted sounds that kept me up all night.

He seemed unmoved by our situation and looked comfortable with the arrangement. I had a different take on our circumstances and desperately wanted a divorce. This was my disaster and mine alone. I had to face it and fix it.

We called an estate agent to list our home on the property market and put our house up for sale, as the payments were falling back. We signed all the documentation in order for the house to be sold.

Everything happened more quickly than I expected. We gave the landscaping a facelift before agents brought potential buyers to the house. We hired garden experts to clean up, trim, and cut down some trees. The lawn also needed some tidying up.

While the workers were trimming a tree in front of the house, one of them silenced the chainsaw to inspect something that he had come across. On investigating, they found a ceramic doll in the tree. The doll was blindfolded and strung up by the neck with a piece of ribbon hanging from one of the branches in the tree.

The doll was attached with a rope to a small toy mattress. As one of the workers inspected the doll on the mattress, he became afraid and flung the doll to the ground.

Judging by his reaction, the man was startled and afraid by this peculiar finding. When I took a turn to inspect their find, I noticed that the doll was pierced with a needle in the side of its leg. The sight was creepy. *How did a doll land in my tree? I certainly did not put it there.*

I found it bizarre that someone would go through all the trouble of placing it there. It must have taken a lot of the person's time and careful planning to accomplish what they'd set up to gain. Wherever the doll came from was a mystery, but the person who'd put it there may have a logical explanation.

One of the workers immediately placed the doll in a box for further investigation. On doing my own research on the day we found it, I came across information on the internet about how people used dolls to curse a certain person they had a grudge against. It also said that such dolls were able to move about on their own while we were asleep.

I was afraid to keep the doll after discovering all that information. It was really scary stuff. I was traumatised as I sat in silence trying to digest these findings and figure out how all this was possible. *Maybe it was placed there before we bought the house, I told myself. Had someone planted the doll for some particular gain?*

My mind was in turmoil, as I remembered passing the tree on numerous occasions and feeling a slight wind that blew but then looking around, only to see that the other trees were still. I'd thought nothing of it at the time—until now. I would never know why the doll was placed there, as I was unable to find any clues as to when it was placed there and by whom.

My mind wandered back to my nightmare when my bed was tied to the tree in the hospital. The tree in my dream and the one in my yard were similar, which I hadn't noticed before now. Once again, it was difficult to distinguish between the reality and the hallucination. The scene before me seemed unbelievably detailed, as it merged with my dream. I simply stared into space, unable to fathom the coincidence.

The very afternoon that we found the doll, we placed the box on the floor, set it alight, and watched as it burned to ashes, as we were afraid to hold on to it any longer. I was suddenly happy that I was leaving all this behind, together with all the bad memories.

The following week, there were people in and out viewing the house. The agent put the house on show over the next few weekends. The problem was, where would we go from here?

It's still early days, I thought to myself. *By the time the sale of the house goes through, we'll have had enough time to make the necessary accommodation plans.* It was time for me to leave my home, even though I had no idea where I was going next.

It had been my home for twenty-two years. Concluding this transaction was going to be one of the saddest occasions of my life. I was not defined by what I did or owned but by what I was leaving behind, I was leaving the safe haven that I'd thought was solid. I did not like what I was going through, especially at this late stage of my life. I was feeling troubled. My plans were out of line and not going according to what was in my mind; my plans were forced to change.

I wallowed in self-pity. I was entitled to feel sorry for myself, as I was at the mercy of the unknown. This was a painful ending for me. I was filled with sorrow, making it impossible to see a new beginning. It was not good for me to harbour resentment because I was not where I expected myself to be. I'd survived through tougher times. I would find another house—a bigger and even better one. I had to strive and become better because of these trying times that were teaching me something at every corner I took. At this point, all I wanted was to move as far away as possible from the painful memories and move to a place where I could start my life over.

Due to a heavy caseload at the Accident Fund, my case continued to drag on and on for what seemed like an eternity. By now, my lawyer, Viola, was carrying around two briefcases full of all my documents to court and back. I became disheartened.

I wanted to cancel the case, but Viola persevered in an effort to finalise my matter by way of settlement out of court at the request of the Fund. The forensic auditor from the Fund who was appointed to assist in trying to settle my case continued to escalate my costs to a high by continuously asking for additional information that had already been given to him on numerous occasions. He proved to be the most ineffective person I'd ever met and seemed uninterested in resolving my matter. He prolonged the case for another year for his own gain.

In the interim, he was paid huge amounts of money. Amid all my frustrations, another auditor was appointed by my lawyer. My case went on for a further year, as the two auditors could not reach an agreement on a settlement figure. My lawyer remained loyal throughout my case. She faithfully kept me updated on the progress.

A decision between the lawyers was made to settle out of court once more, but still, they could not reach an agreement. The case was once more left in the air, unfinished.

14

I ought to keep going even though my world was turned upside down. My mind was telling me that I should be happy with my life and that I must stop objecting needlessly. But this world I was living in was opposing me. It kept throwing curveballs at me. I suppose I wanted adventure, but I got it in a different form than I was expecting. I was in the wrong place at the wrong time, but I believed that one day, when I least expected it, an opportunity might present itself. I would no longer be saying 'poor me'. I resolved that my trials would not slow me down or stop me. If anything, they would move me forward to new and greater lengths.

Through my trials, I'd been taught that pain came with a purpose—to see how strong I really was, even when I was running on empty. I'd learned to wait and became aware of what was more important in my life. It had taught me to persevere. This was all part of God's work.

Anthony continued to be on his phone for what seemed to be every minute of the day. When I glanced at him, he was constantly engrossed in his phone, making sure that his screen was out of my line of vision. Everything about his phone was top secret. His phone always remained locked. It was hidden in his back pocket when not in his hand.

Something was not making sense, but I just could not put my finger on anything specific.

I opted to pry through his belongings to find distinct evidence to back my agitation. This time around, no one would stop me if I had the evidence I needed. He continued to disappear at odd times of the day. He often left home without so much as an explanation, though, if pressed, he always invented credible excuses, if a bit flimsy. He often said that he was going to spend time with friends. This seemed odd because all his friends were still at work at that time of the day.

One evening he arrived home late. I questioned him about his whereabouts. He simply replied, 'Out.' The vagueness of his response gave me no comfort. I kept getting an agitated feeling.

I grew tired of his games, which turned out to be annoying. It appeared as if he was the only player in the game having fun. The fear that resulted from his actions kept catching me off guard, but I refused to let this enemy called fear control my life. I was supposed to be in control.

It was time to dig deep to find what was making me uneasy. Suspicions led me to search for tangible evidence all over again; I needed clues that would lead me to his deceit and lies. I wanted anything to verify the fact that he had gone astray yet again. I could not live this lie anymore. I wanted out of this decomposed marriage. Instead of standing together through our difficult times, we stood divided, and we were doomed to fall.

The idea that he was cheating left a sick feeling in the pit of my stomach, especially after all the sincere promises he'd made.

Determined to find something, I set out to become my own private investigator, trusting my instincts. I searched through his pockets but found nothing. I went into his garage to search through his car — still nothing. I searched the boot of his car.

There it was, staring back at me — a box containing a brand-new phone with wrapping paper beside it. There was a tight feeling in my throat as I tried to swallow. I held the box in my hand as I read the card. 'To Avril.'

I peeked into the box, noticing that it contained a very expensive phone. I placed the box back where I'd found it. I also found a receipt for an expensive electrical stove, which did not enter into my house. I then closed the boot.

I did not want to accept what I'd seen and tried to make excuses. In my mind, I was in denial. It seemed as though someone had punched me in the stomach and knocked the wind out of me.

As I entered the lounge, his phone lit up and made a beeping sound. I picked it up. He had been unusually negligent by forgetting his phone on the table. The odds were in my favour, as he was careless.

I read the message that popped up on the screen: 'I miss you so much, can we please meet tomorrow?' it read, followed by a heart sign. The message was from Avril. I browsed through his phone. There were many phone calls and text messages between them.

The red flag of unfaithfulness was once more revealed. It did not call for further proof, as I now had all the facts that I needed in my hand. I did not waste any more time approaching him. I was furious and chose to question him about my discovery. I'd guessed that he was hiding something all along; my suspicions had just been confirmed.

At the same time, I was troubled by my discovery, as I'd trusted him when he'd told me he would never go back to her. I got the feeling that they had never separated in the first place.

'Anthony, you have a message,' I informed him calmly as I handed him his phone.

His face went blood red, but at the same time, he pretended to be composed and gave me a silly shrug. There was an awkward silence in the air as he read his message. I tried to keep my temper in control, but his next reaction startled me.

'I have no idea why she is sending me messages, as I have not seen her in ages. I haven't been in contact with her in a long time.'

'If you have not seen her in ages, why is she sending you messages that tell a different story?'

'I haven't the slightest idea.' His voice lowered. 'Why don't you believe me when I say it's over between me and Avril? I've stopped all my nonsense. Can't you see I am a new person?'

His lies sounded so shallow that my ears actually hurt. *He must really think I'm an idiot, as he constantly insults my intelligence,* I speculated. I was surprised by the ease with which he lied. Lies were not a wise move on his side, as I had seen the proof for myself.

'What about the inappropriate message that just came through on your phone?' I stood there with a tight feeling in my throat, fighting back the tears that were threatening to stream down my cheeks. I prepared myself for his reaction and knew that he was likely to be in denial, even though I presented him with the evidence. At this stage, I chose to be hurt by the truth, rather than to be 'comforted' with more of his lies.

'I'm not sure why she is still sending me messages, as I have not seen or heard from her in a long time,' he repeated, not knowing what else to say. His behaviour continued to undermine me. He gave the word 'liar' a new meaning. I was caught up in this web of deception.

'If you want to convince anyone of your lie, you need to learn to convince yourself first. I want out of this marriage that has been built on a lie.' I could not help raising my voice. I was at a total loss for words. Even though I had the facts, my thoughts were still uncertain of making the wrong decision. I could not think straight.

Despite the evidence I'd presented to him, I still wanted a confession from him. But at the same time, I was hoping that he would come up with an excuse to convince me that it was not true.

Unexpectedly, like he was grasping at straws, he turned around to face me and, then looked me straight in the eye. 'If Jesus can forgive, why can't you?' His voice was filled with accusation as he proclaimed his innocence in his wrongdoing.

'Clearly, I am not Jesus,' I blurted.

'You spend so much time praying, but you are unforgiving and wicked. I don't think you know how to pray!' He confessed to his actions and then turned it all on me.

'How dare you think you are in a position to judge me about my time spent in prayer?' I asked furiously. I had difficulty looking into his face. 'You have treated me with such malice and disrespect these past few years. What have I done to you that was so terrible that warranted all these affairs with these different women? Please make me understand. I have put up with your betrayal and your lies, pretending all was well. Why did you stay if you were so unhappy?' The questions could not stop.

He seemed very uncomfortable by my probing. The silence was like a death sentence as I paused, waiting for a response, which never came. Luckily, the children had gone out for the day.

'The way you acted out your anger in the presence of our children was unacceptable; your temper always got the better of you. I tried my best to please you, but nothing I ever did was good enough for you.'

'You've changed too,' he retaliated with a stubborn look on his face.

'If I was doing something out of place, why didn't you bring it to my attention? It still does not explain why you had to seek out other women for company; you owe it to me to tell me the truth!'

'The affairs made me feel younger again,' he eventually blurted out arrogantly. I caught a smirk on his face.

I couldn't believe what I heard. His ego needed some boosting!

He was putting me down. I was belittled by his proclamation. My self-esteem was destroyed. I was infuriated because it sounded like an accusation against me. He strayed from the straight and narrow because he needed his ego to be boosted! I did not have the energy to listen to any more of his garbage.

I turned to walk away. I was weary as I sank deep into my chair, listening to the sounds of the crickets chirping away. I was rattled by our confrontation. The unexpected cruel twist of fate was a blow as I thought of starting over this late in my life.

There was one more thing I had to do. When everyone was asleep, I mustered up the courage to call Avril. I had taken her number down the day I saw her messages on Anthony's phone. My hands were shaking as I began to dial her number.

'Hello. This is Avril.'

I heard her introduce herself politely as she answered her phone. Her voice sounded very familiar, like I had spoken to her before, but I could not link the voice to a specific person. I began to breathe unevenly, not knowing what to say. My nerves were about to snap.

'This is Hannah, Anthony's wife. I hope my call does not come as a shock to you. I'm sure I don't exist in your world, but you exist in mine since I found out about you through your messages to my husband. I would like to know exactly what your connection with Anthony is. Let's be straight with each other, so do not lie to me.

He has already confessed his unfaithfulness to me, but I wanted to hear your side of this messy affair.' I held my breath.

'We are only friends —' She started with her denial.

'Come on. Don't bullshit me. I am not that ignorant!' I spat out.

'He disclosed that you don't make him happy anymore and that he was going to ask you for a divorce, as he is no longer in love with you.'

I was shattered as I listened while she brought me up to date, but I was not prepared to give her power over me. My own self-respect felt torn to shreds, however.

'Don't you dare patronise me. He needs to confront me himself to tell me how he feels. Or are you his spokesperson? I hope he will make you happy, because, once a cheat, always a cheater.' I fumbled for words, not knowing quite what to say.

'At the beginning I did not know that he was married. When I learnt that he had a family, I tried to break it off.'

'Don't bother; you deserve each other,' I blurted, filled with annoyance. She offered more personal information than I expected to hear, which startled me. I was trembling with anger as I replaced the receiver in its cradle. I stared at the phone for a long time, not knowing how to move forward. I was disappointed in myself for having contacted her. His betrayal made me react in an uncharacteristic way that was beneath me. I did not approve of what I done. We all do things we don't want to do. I behaved in a way that I never believed was possible by contacting her.

My frustration mounted, and she became the target for a lot of my resentment. She made me feel rage such as I'd never felt before. My mind went wild with unhealthy thoughts. I'd assumed phoning her would make me feel better, but it did not; instead, my head was reeling out of control.

He discussed my family life with her. She knew a lot about my life—personal matters I only share with my close friends and family. She knew about Stephanie's pregnancy and that she had twins. She even knew when Kiara was born. This affair must have been going on since before my accident! This was about as bad as it could get.

My back was against the wall with limited options as I began to think of how to proceed to the next stage. I closed my eyes for a moment and conjured up a mental picture of her. Was she pretty? Was she slim? But I quickly wiped those thoughts out of my mind before they made me sick. The familiarity of her voice did not make sense to me at all, because I'd never met or spoken to her before today. But her voice kept bugging me.

I searched deep into my mind to track it down. My blood literally went cold as my memory was triggered. I Remembered hearing her voice while I was in a coma. How was that possible, because my family had been there all the time? I recognised her voice, but I could not share this piece of information with anyone, as I did not have any concrete evidence. Could she be the woman with the strange voice? The possibilities were boundless, all I could do was pay close attention by silently observing my surroundings like I never had before. What more could possibly still go wrong?

I was terrified by my discovery. It felt as though the pain would never end.

Upon doing some prying of my own, I learnt that Avril had lost her first husband, and her second husband had divorced her. She was the sole supporter of her family, struggling with two adult boys who did not work. I could not help but feel pity for her. It was obvious now why Anthony did not support his family financially.

He had to take care of his supposedly new family!

Many thoughts continued to pop into my head. I was trying to cling to this person who did not care for me anymore. It was my moment of shame. I was emotionally numb, and just stood there, somehow feeling no pain, that was the worst pain. I was living through the nastiest experience of my life, as the same scene played out in my mind.

I gave careful consideration to my next move. More importantly, I had to think about me. I did not want to act out of impulse. I needed to do what was right for me.

When we were alone, I approached him after our morning meal and made sure to convey my request with caution, as I enlightened him that my mind was made up and that I wanted to go ahead with the divorce. There was no more backing out or negotiating on this subject. We had reached a point of no return. The same pattern kept repeating itself. Now was the time to change it.

'I have been thinking about our marriage. I feel that our situation has not improved despite all the efforts I have made. Every option of trying to save our marriage has been worn out. I really don't see any other choice at this point, as we are both unhappy. It is undeniably best for us to go ahead with the divorce and go our separate ways.'

He was silent; for a long time, he did not respond.

'I feel so betrayed by someone I trusted and loved and to whom I dedicated the best years of my life. We have been living apart for years, sleeping in separate rooms. Up until now, I did not see reason to act upon the situation, in the hope that you would reconsider and change your selfishness.'

I left the room, giving him time to think about what I'd said.

This was a decision I didn't want to make at my age. Instead, I kept avoiding it for a long time.

'Don't walk out on me please. I deserve another chance,' he pleaded, walking behind me. 'I will prove to you that I can change. I know I have not been the husband that I ought to be. I have been working on my temper and on my drinking. I promise the affairs will stop.'

His words sounded so false it was unbelievably tiring. I was stunned that he even attempted to validate his actions. He was shaken about the divorce and wanted to make the usual empty promises. Anthony finally grasped the seriousness of the matter and made every effort to defend himself. As usual, he acted in his own arrogance.

"Your infidelity has been going on for over ten years. Why will it be different this time around? I have given you so many chances, but you wouldn't stop to reconsider the options that would be good for us. You will never change; this is who you are. Why did you think that our family was not worth saving?' I demanded.

I saw the tears roll down his eyes. I was not sure whether they were tears of shame or remorse or maybe even happiness.

'I have given it a lot of thought. I have come to the conclusion that you no longer need me; it has been clear to me for a long time.

You just like the idea of us being together—the security, being served, your laundry being done, just to name a few. The love is gone, so don't strain yourself on my account with false promises,' I continued.

'You know what the awful thing about all this is? I never suspected it in the beginning. When I eventually saw the signs and the evidence, I looked the other way, thinking it was a passing phase because I was hopeful and really thought that you may change your bad habits. But you chose not to. You just carried on.' My words continued to flow out, and I meant every word I said.

'I gave you so many chances in the past. Six affairs later, that I am aware of, and you are still asking me to forgive and forget?'

I was amazed. 'Why the hell didn't you leave me, since you have been telling everyone that you had intentions of divorcing me? You even went as far as telling Megan that you are going to leave me as soon as my leg was healed. Why did you stay?'

At least he had the decency to wait for my leg to heal, I reasoned sarcastically. This time, the tears were rolling down my cheeks.

My mind was made up. There was nothing anyone could do to change it. Our marriage had become a sham. I did not have the energy to go up against him anymore. The wheels of justice had been delayed for a long time; it was time for them to turn in my support. I had to do what was good for me.

'By the way,' I added, 'I saw the package in the boot of your car. I really hope she enjoys the gift and all the many other gifts that you have given her. To think you never contributed towards the children's education for the past six years — not even towards the running expenses in the home. You left it all to me. You relinquished all responsibility towards your family. What kind of a man does that?' I whispered.

'You know what is so strange? I was faithful to you no matter what the situation turned out to be. There were so many opportunities for me to deceive you, but I chose to remain faithful because I valued what we had. If we had to spin the wheel around, would you be able to forgive me?'

He remained silent, as if it was a struggle to talk.

I had sacrificed my own needs by pleasing everyone around me and not considering what I needed. I watched my life fade away. There was no longer us but me. My days ahead were looking even darker. I would do something for me, by giving myself some time to connect with my inner self and finally letting go of all the pain.

I tried to keep the ordeal of handling the divorce to a minimum for the sake of the children. I was terrified of making the wrong decision, yet I desperately wanted to do what was true for me and my future. Their lives would change drastically by being separated from their father. I wanted to be sensitive towards them and for them to remain anchored, as I knew that the divorce was a fragile issue that would cause them tremendous anxiety. They would be upset emotionally and may even hate me, but there was no easy way out of this.

I was forced to deal with the consequences of my actions, but right now I had to restore normality back into my life. Over time the uncertainties should dissolve; furthermore, they ought to adapt to the changes.

I tried to rewind to ten years ago, to the time my marriage began to fail, but I was unable to see that far back. I could feel that I was not the same person anymore. My mind was in overdrive, as I was forced to consider certain aspects of my life. I had not signed up for all this turbulence I was going through. He had taken something from me, and I needed to get it back — my dignity.

15

I lay in bed filled with sadness, staring into space in the night, remembering everything that took place, replaying the conversations in my mind, thinking about every discussion, reflecting on the hurtful dialogue. I paused to consider what I was leaving behind to start from scratch all on my own. The agony of saying goodbye to my old life and accepting my reality felt overwhelming. All these thoughts forced me to assess my priorities once more. I was worried about my future and thinking of how distraught I was by Anthony's disloyalty. I began to question my sanity and speculated about why he'd had these affairs, why he'd treated me so unkindly.

Was I to blame? Did I drive him to seek other women? Will I make it on my own? I needed to process all these hurtful experiences that had led to my current situation. I reminded myself that I made a sensible move. Forgiveness was not going to take place overnight. However, the idea of the divorce began to take a serious toll on my well-being. I became exceedingly uncomfortable as I worked through my feelings, while figuring out what I truly wanted.

I had to deal with this in a logical way. The distasteful occurrences were upsetting, but my intelligence told me that my decision was long overdue. It took me a long time to see through him and react to his deceptions. It was expected that my whole world would be altered, as I was sacrificing my stable life and giving up my place of safety to step into a new world. The sense of watching my world fall apart before my eyes was crushing. However, I would not lose hope. I would take whatever bold action was required from me to better my position. It was time to stop feeling sorry for myself. My main aim was to separate myself from my past and trust that things would unfold as they should.

My day began like every other day. I woke up to a fresh cup of coffee made by Anthony, as he did for me every morning. I took a sip; it tasted rather strange. My tongue was numb. I felt dizzy and spent the day in bed. *Perhaps I ate something that upset me. Surely the coffee was not responsible for making me ill? No, he wouldn't!*

By the time evening came, I was feeling better. I thought I must be coming down with a bug or with some kind of virus.

Two days later, he made me coffee once more. I made toast to go with it, but once again, I felt dizzy. This time, my stomach became upset. I was in agonising pain. I spent the rest of the day throwing up in the bathroom.

I was rushed to the hospital casualty, as my nausea and stomach pain persisted. After many blood tests, including examinations, the doctors could not find anything wrong with me. I was put onto a drip, but my symptoms seemed to worsen. By now I was panicking.

I was admitted into hospital for further observation. Anthony left me at the hospital. I learned later that he informed my family that I was stable and that it was not necessary for them to come pop in to see me. Megan and Colleen were confused by this information because of the condition they'd seen me in earlier.

They insisted on coming through to the hospital to make sure that I was in good health.

History seemed to be repeating itself. They were horrified to find me in a critical state, with the doctors rushing around my bed. I was delirious and had an excruciating headache. I was drenched with perspiration as the doctors ran further tests and drew more blood from my veins, but they were unable to trace the cause of my illness. All the tests that they ran came back normal.

One of the doctors enquired from me whether I could raise enough funds to do intense testing, as the benefits from my medical fund did not cover the particular tests they wanted to run.

I responded that I did not have the amount of money they requested. I watched as the doctor flicked through my file with a surprised look on her face and insinuated that there was a good chance that someone might have given me something to eat or drink. She suggested that someone in my company was very naughty. *What exactly was she implying?*

My blood went cold. She really didn't have to say more. I read between the lines and made my own assumptions. It did not need a lot of imagination to know the inevitable. How was it possible that the doctors could not diagnose my condition and, furthermore, were strangely unable to identify my illness or even make a close diagnosis?

Instead, I was treated for flu and for an ear and throat infection. One of the doctors implied that the dizziness I was experiencing was caused by loose crystals in my inner ear.

Yet, the doctor's comment raised many questions in my mind. I was convinced that someone might have given me something to eat or drink against my will. I had no proof that anything of the sort had happened, but the mystery had me thinking deeply.

I was fortunate because I managed to survive the ordeal. Whatever the individual's intentions were, the plan seemed to have collapsed because I was still breathing! I had once more cheated death.

When my kids came to the hospital that Sunday, they all looked very uncomfortable. I asked what was bothering them, but they remained edgy.

Stephanie eventually blurted out, 'Mom, Robyn heard Dad speaking to someone on the phone. He made arrangements to meet whoever it was during the course of the day.'

'Who was he talking to?' I asked curiously.

'At first Robyn thought he was talking to you, but as the conversation went on, she concluded that it was someone else. Before ending the call, he told the person how much he loves her and that you were in hospital.'

In a strange way, the information did not upset me as it would have previously. I told them not to worry about it. When I got home after being discharged from the hospital, I was extra careful with what I ate or drank. I could not live a life of constantly having to look over my shoulder to see what unscrupulous act was going to strike me. I was afraid that, out of desperation, Anthony might allow his infidelity to influence his actions and do something fatal to me.

At the same time, I convinced myself that he would never harm me. Even if I thought that, I also somehow knew that it was worth paying attention, not because I was afraid, but because my life seemed under threat. Looking away or being ignorant at this stage could be crucial.

Back home, I retired to my room. I was standing by my bedroom window and listened to the wind howling when I noticed a shadow lurking under my door in the darkness. There was a deep silence as the shadow stayed briefly before it moved away. Cold chills moved down my spine, as all kinds of thoughts went through my mind. The moment felt like forever. I was afraid and wanted to hide but was simultaneously unable to move, being rooted to the spot. I wondered who lurked by my bedroom door. Was it one of the children or maybe even an intruder?

The following day, I learned that it was Anthony, who was getting water to drink from the kitchen. Why did he linger by my door for a while? Maybe he wanted to discuss the day's events and then suddenly changed his mind.

Morning came. I was once again presented with a cup of coffee made by Anthony. I informed him that I did not drink coffee anymore.

He took the cup and shoved it at me. 'You will drink it. I've been making you coffee for the past thirty years,' he insisted firmly.

I was obliged to take the cup of coffee from him. Later, when he was gone, I poured it down the basin in the bathroom.

I became uncomfortable in his presence; there was no predicting what he had up his sleeve. Nor did I have proof that he or anyone had attempted to do the unexplained. Like a dark cloud in the distance warning that a storm was imminent, so was my gut feeling warning me to be cautious! This may sound crazy, but I was terrified to eat or drink anything given to me by anyone. I became paranoid and started imagining things. I remained silent about it all though because I assumed my suspicions were unfounded, and therefore, my concerns were invalid.

I had been married to this person for more than thirty years, and he turned out to be a stranger to me. He transformed overnight. I did not know him anymore. Deception can be brutal. I found myself grieving for my past and mourning for the future I'd thought we were creating together. I was nervous to confront him because of his history of violence. I never knew when his disruptive behaviour would rear its head. Even though the violence diminished over the years, my thoughts consciously drew me back to the past, so I decided to remain silent.

The days turned into weeks. Megan and I met at a coffee bar to spend some time together.

'How are you coping with the situation at home Hannah? You seem distracted. Did you sleep well?'

'Look at me; I'm a wreck,' I replied, giving her an account of the past weeks' misfortunes. I briefed her on everything that the doctor had implied when I was in hospital with that mysterious illness.

She was speechless. Her advice was for me to speed up the divorce, settle for the best price on the house, and cut all ties immediately.

'I have no proof that my drinks or my food have been interfered with, but how do you explain what happened to me? I am hardly a sickly person.' My suspicions were unsupported at this point, as I did not have the evidence to back me up. I presumed that my mistrustful thoughts caused me to imagine everything.

'Do you remember the day we overheard him speaking to his friend Benjamin?' I stirred up her memory.

'Yes, I do. I wanted to refresh your memory too but chose not to. I thought you'd erased it from your mind, so I did not want to upset you further.'

'How could I forget when all three of us heard the discussion clearly? His friend asked him if he was prepared to wait until my money from the fund is released or whether he would go ahead with divorcing me.'

'Yes, his response was that he was willing to wait for the money. It appears as if your assumptions are true. The facts are presenting themselves. Walk around with your eyes and your ears opened, as I know you can be very trusting at times,' warned Megan.

'Always remember that premeditated murders come from people who are very close to us — those people have very shifty intentions in their minds and plan their actions carefully before they act. However, no one is free from the consequences of his or her choices, and it will catch up with the person concerned. The individual involved seems to want power and control over all you have worked for. When I think of all you've been through, it makes my blood boil that someone may be trying to hurt you. Don't ever let your guard down.' Megan looked very serious as she offered her point of view.

We stayed at the coffee bar a long time expressing our thoughts about the inexplicable mysteries that were unfolding in my life. Who would do such a thing and what was their motive? These things happen on television, not to me. We came back to the fact that I could not explain or prove any of the occurrences. Anything was a possibility. I had to be alert. I was let down and dreaded the idea of going back home. I always gave the world the impression that all was good, walking around responding to people with false smiles on my face, as if my life was problem free. No one knew what was going on behind closed doors or the emotional abuse I endured. Who knew what my fate would be next time if someone *was* actually intent on doing me harm or destroying my life? Someone seems to think that my life was not worth living. I went home feeling very unbalanced and knew that I had to respond more carefully to situations that were making me feel unsafe.

Over the next few weeks, I was in and out of the offices of my lawyers who were attending to the divorce. My nephew Renaldo, gave me the support I needed and urged me to think carefully before making my final decision, but my mind was made up. I could not believe that I had made this painful decision to end our marriage. It took a lot of courage to dive into this unpleasant split-up, as I had been putting it off for many years. I eventually plucked up the courage to go ahead with it. I was a few days shy of being free from the unpleasant relationship that had upset my life for so many years. He did not contest the divorce. He willingly signed all the documentation when it was presented to him.

During the divorce proceedings I could sense his intense anger towards me. I appeared in court a week later after he signed the papers, and the divorce was settled. I was relieved that it was over with and that I could start my new life as an officially single woman. I set him free and, at the same time, liberated myself.

My fate was decided. I accepted it gracefully, even though it came with a price—a very high price of thirty-odd years of my time, hard work, and effort that I'd put into the marriage. It was futile to regret my decision, as the bad marriage had already consumed too many years of my life. I did not want to waste any more time on regret. Everything changed in an instant for me. I had not signed up for all his cheating, lies, and unhappiness. It was good to be free from this fake relationship. I was not perfect; I had my flaws and had made wrong decisions and some mistakes during my life, but only time would tell how my life would still evolve. What mattered to me was that I had taken the positive step to a happier life, and I had the resilience to pick myself up. I would deal with the aftermath of these changes as they came.

When he received the news that we were legally divorced, Anthony's temper once again got the better of him, and he began to scream. He lashed out at the children. Every tasteless word in the dictionary was flung at me. He tried to shift the blame onto my daughters, accusing them of knowing about my intentions to file for a divorce. He also insinuated that I'd discussed it with them and that they could have given him the heads-up. He made himself the innocent victim by looking for someone to blame for his shortcomings. It was easier to blame someone than to face his own reality. He was afraid to admit his wrongdoing and wanted the children to carry a part of the blame for knowing about the divorce. Maybe this was a cry for support from the children, but if it was, he was going about it the wrong way.

'Why did you not tell me that your mother was going to divorce me? I could have stopped the divorce if I knew about it in time,' he kept yelling at them.

I expressed that the divorce had been underway for a long time; no one was to blame but himself. I'd discussed the divorce with him anyway, but he evidently thought I was calling his bluff.

'Relationships never die on their own you know. It took *you* to destroy it. Our marriage broke because of lies, cheating, and lack of respect.' I informed him.

He continued saying terribly hurtful things, but I just ignored him. I did not want to give him the benefit of the doubt of knowing how his words affected me.

'We had a beautiful life when we started out, but you were the one who chose to go astray. Admit your faults and accept that you were wrong. Maybe then you will be able to see the bigger picture instead of trying to push the blame onto everyone else.'

He remained silent as I spoke.

'I am sorry that we got divorced and for everything bad that happened in our lives, but it was always about you, not about us. You are the one who decided to seek the company of someone else by giving up on our marriage. Man up. Don't go around blaming everyone for what has taken place. You milled whatever was good between us.' I tried my best to exercise control as I spoke.

He seemed to be holding me responsible for the damage of our marriage and forgot that there were consequences for his choices. Maybe this was a natural reaction for him, but I needed to make sense of why he was acting so surprised and blaming everyone around him.

He spent the next hour on the phone broadcasting the news to his friends and family, updating them on the divorce and telling them that he was officially single. I could not understand his anger because he was the one who'd expressed dissatisfaction with the marriage by choosing to be disloyal.

'Thirty years down the tube. You destroyed this marriage, always trying to make yourself better!' he kept shouting for the whole neighbourhood to hear.

I heard the sound of dishes and cutlery being flung around in the kitchen. When Colleen and Robyn heard the commotion, they left in the hope that we might settle our differences. I was afraid to be left alone with him; unfortunately, I had no choice but to face the music. At the same time, I was relieved that they would not be exposed to his cruel verbal attacks. I kept my distance from him, but I was also glad to have the helper in the background should anything happen to me.

She remained in the background and, occasionally, I heard her announce, 'God help us!'

He called me horrible names. When he was finished degrading me, he got into his car and left in a great haste. The car's tyres screeched as he drove off, and I let out a sigh of relief. I remained prepared and ready for his next move, as I could not bear to be caught unawares.

My nerves were on edge when he arrived a few hours later with all his friends, already half intoxicated. I'd somewhat expected the drama that followed. I sensed trouble by the way he spoke; his body language told me even more. This was the start of my nightmare. His family also showed up at my house. The fun and games were about to begin. I did not have to be part of it.

I could just imagine the false gossips that he must have told them about me, as most of them just looked at me with not even as much as an acknowledgment. They continued walking to the entertainment area, each holding a different type of beverage in his or her hands. The music began to blast so loudly that the windows in the kitchen rattled. Sympathy drinking was going to take place. The sooner I left, the better.

My helper packed a weekend bag and left for the weekend, not wanting to be part of the racket. *Buckle up. It's going to be a jagged ride*, I carefully considered as I grabbed my bag, bolting for the door as the children arrived to pick me up.

I left the house before any drama could take place. My son in-law, William, joined Anthony in the hope of consoling him.

Later in the evening, William phoned sounding nervous as he warned me about the unpleasant situation that was going down.

'It is not advisable to come home now. Anthony is intoxicated and angry. His friends are planting ideas into his head and giving him drunken advice. He may become violent, and he is not in control of his actions,' William cautioned with an unsteady voice.

We ordered takeaways for dinner and then found a quiet place on the Hill Top View. We stayed there for most of the evening. The sight from the top was stunning, and the lights were glowing brightly, but I was unable to appreciate the scenic beauty in front of me. I stood at the lookout point viewing my surroundings from the top and, at the same time, observing my own state of mind. The stillness of the night allowed my mind to dwell on what was taking place and Anthony's anger, together with the many questions that were going through my mind. There was a chill in the night air.

William phoned again and suggested that we fetch the key to his house and that we should stay at his place till he called again. By the time midnight struck, William phoned again to tell us that Anthony was asleep and that the coast was clear, as all his guests had left. We were relieved as we made our way home, quietly entering the house.

He awoke at midday, appearing calm, as if he'd digested and accepted the divorce. Could it be the calm before the storm? That remained to be seen.

The next few weeks became very uncomfortable, as we had to face each other, sometimes spending time in the same room.

Soon after, everything started falling into place. The agent found a buyer. I was pleased that the house was sold. The price was not what we were expecting, but we took the offer anyway, as we were both in a hurry to go our separate ways.

I heard a knock on the door late on Saturday afternoon. To my surprise, there stood Megan. It was a pleasant surprise, as I'd seldom had company these last few days. We went into the kitchen, where I made a pot of tea. We made ourselves comfortable and discussed our individual ventures.

'There seem to have been many terrible ordeals taking place over the past few years in your life, Hannah,' Megan pointed out after some time.

'I have no idea why my life has changed so drastically. I have made it my duty to embrace each experience and learn from every hardship. Life has been difficult—the affairs, the accident, Colleen's ordeal, losing the business, being unemployed, having to sell my home, and the divorce, just to mention a few. It really is a great deal to process at once. It's been one catastrophe after the other,' I replied sadly.

Too many things had gone wrong in many different ways, I thought with discouragement. Maybe God was angry with me.

I was unable to find the meaning to my suffering or even see the hidden lessons. I was not spared. My plate was overflowing. The thought suddenly brought tears to my eyes.

These days, the tears flowed easily. I could not control them. Everyone's story has a bit of sorrow, but mine had plenty.

'What can I do to improve my life so that it can become easier?' I asked Megan, turning to look at her, hoping to find answers.

'I'm sorry for what you're experiencing right now. There seems to be some horrid unknown force hovering in your life. Remember God's plan never fails. Do not get disheartened. When you go to church, pray for the removal of all evil that is operating in your life and for what is beyond your ability to control. Don't worry about anything. Just ask God for what you need and always be thankful when you pray, not forgetting to ask for forgiveness. Never cease praying.' Megan continued to be supportive, giving me the courage to move forward, and at the same time, her presence was a healing one for me. She somehow had the heart for making things better.

'I rebuke any evil from my life and I send it straight to' — as I looked around for the closest thing to me to point at, just then the dog walked past—'to this old brown dog!' I said, pointing and making a playful joke.

We both laughed at the joke.

An hour later, Megan went home. Robyn assisted me as I fed the dogs.

Just as we were ready to settle in for the night, the dog came up to us for a goodnight pat on the head, as he always did. We both screamed at the same time, making a dash to get on the other side of the gate as we noticed that the pupils of the dog's eyes had changed to a strange dark yellow. We continued to stare at the dog through the gate as he began to snarl at us. His actions were far from normal. The dog did not respond as we called to him; he continued to howl and stared directly at us. The other dog picked up the howling too. Both dogs howled continuously throughout the night. It was a very eerie sound that gave me the shivers. I went about my duties of locking the doors as usual and preparing to go to bed. I lay awake in bed listening to the noise.

'What is happening to the dogs? They are freaking me out!' Robyn appeared in my room looking startled.

I reassured her that the dogs were just agitated and that she should return to bed.

When I awoke the following morning, I was taken aback when I found the brown dog lying dead near the kitchen door and the black dog sitting close to his companion. Guilt filled my heart as I remembered my silly joke.

How could I have made such a distasteful joke? My thoughts flashed back to the hospital when the two dogs were marching up and down in my ward. What was the connection between my dream and this incident with the dogs? The visions were becoming more realistic than ever before. I was determined to find the answers.

Had my dreams been warning me about something? Or was it just a bad coincidence? Was there really an evil spirit lurking in my life? Had it been transferred to the dog? My mind was way overstretched.

I phoned Megan to tell her what had happened. Was I to blame because of what I'd said? She insisted that it had nothing to do with our conversation, even though I knew deep down that, as the saying goes, 'The tongue is a powerful weapon.'

My memory went back to my nightmares in hospital, which all seemed to be coming to light—the selling of body parts, the fraud in my business that related to the missing money in the train, the bed and the tree episode, and now the dogs! I became tense, thinking back to my horrible nightmares.

A few days later, we were very sad when the other dog died with symptoms that were unknown. Wicked thoughts about the entire situation filled my mind, as I was caught up in a dark twist of bad fortune. Maybe I would be cut some slack and my problems will ease.

It took a whole week to complete our packing and divide our possessions in half. I made sure that Anthony received everything he needed to start up his new home. We kept the process as amicable as possible to avoid upsetting the children. To keep the process from becoming a contentious battle, our assets were split down the middle. Everything that he was legally entitled to was given to him. I did not want to drag this mess out by holding back on whatever he requested. I wanted this chaos to be over and done with.

The children helped him look for suitable accommodation but one of his friends offered him a cottage that was on his premises. I was relieved that he would not be living alone. We also found a house to rent, and then we went our separate ways.

I know that God never promised that life would be easy, but He did promise that He would always be at my side, no matter how difficult and trying my situation turned out to be. *Will I ever adjust? Will I get used to this?* I wondered as the tears of distress started all over again, and it all began to sink in.

Unfortunately, life is not fair. Tragedies strike our lives at some point or the other. The right decisions were not written in a book for me to know what would take place after all this.

Right now, I was on a journey with no destination. But somehow, I considered that I was on my way to where I was supposed to be. I was doing okay. It would get better; it normally does. Bad things happen to everyone; I was no different. My choice was either to sit around and mope or shake off the loss of my marriage. There were a lot of 'what ifs' on my mind that kept unsettling me.

All I could do was pray as I made plans for my future. It was difficult not to feel anxious at the thought of starting from the beginning on my own. It was not an option for me to accept defeat and hide. I had to get back up and be the fighter I once was and fight to overcome these many ordeals facing me. I finally closed the chapter that disturbed my life.

I would never get the years back from my past, but I was free from the chains of pretending that all was sunny and bright. Like the saying goes, 'Running water does not flow back.' It's the same with life; it's happened. I was driven by hope. It was time to create my own fate.

Over the years, I'd lived with guilt, avoiding the truth of my failed marriage. But in the end, I was fooling myself because *I* ended up becoming the miserable one. I doubt that our marriage could have lasted another month, let alone another year. The divorce was painful on both of us, mentally and physically. I'd been taught valuable lessons, good and bad. Some of the negative experiences were overpowering the good and refused to go away, but in the end, they'd also helped me to acquire more wisdom.

I grew up overnight from all that had happened. I suddenly got that heightened feeling that there was no place I could call my home. I was wandering on an unknown road, with just my faith my pocket.

16

I'd reflected about the events of those terrible months so often and so deeply, it was time to let go. My depression took my thoughts back to my parents. If only they were alive, my mother would have given me the guidance that I needed or directed me on how to handle this awful mess I was in. I had every reason to be proud of myself for taking the step to leave my old abusive life behind. In a blink of an eye, I had become a stranger to myself; not knowing who I was, left me with a hollow emptiness inside. Like everything else in life, I was compelled to adjust to the changes and get to the point of accepting my past. My loneliness caught up with me. I felt disconnected, as if I was cut off from everyone else. The temptation to consume a bottle of wine and irrigate my problems for a while was great, but I chose not to, as the following day, they would still be there.

My daily routine was put to the test. The unwelcome emotional state of leaving my old life behind made me struggle to regain my usual rhythm. I needed to establish new habits in order to get the familiar ones out of my mind. I needed to keep busy in an attempt to lose my troubled thoughts. I was operating on autopilot, doing things needlessly. Having to swim against the tide was exhausting.

I had entered into a place in my life that I did not understand. This was a path I'd never travelled on before, but

I was headed in the right direction. I had survived yesterday, and with God's help, I would harvest the right seeds for my tomorrow.

In an effort to keep busy and hoping to lose my fretful thoughts, I decided that walking might be helpful to possibly improve on my dull mood. I preferred to stroll around in the mall and walk off all the negativity I was feeling. I wandered from shop to shop looking at all the displays of bags, shoes, and outfits through the shop windows. As I looked at all the clothing, I could not help but think about the changes I was still trying to adapt to. I decided that, for now, I would rather think of the many choices I had, instead of looking at the choices I could not have. It may just dampen my mood further.

I hoped to purchase a few items to lift my spirits, but I did not spot anything that caught my attention. *Retail therapy is not working in my favour today*, I determined. With my mind being so distant, I walked around the mall twice and reached the end of the shopping centre. I decided to go back home, as I was feeling no better after my leisurely walk. I scarcely noticed the roads as I made my way back to my rented house. I arrived home and spent the day reading to occupy my mind.

Fifty-two years old and starting a new life alone! The thought of being by myself made me feel sad. But at the same time, I looked forward to my new life ahead, full of challenges and rediscovering who I was. This was my life beginning in a new way. I would make time for all the people and things that I neglected. Each day given to me was a blessing. I would welcome each new day as a fresh opportunity to learn from the experiences I've been through.

I was here now, and I was not about to let my age limit me; neither would my situation set me back. Instead, my mistakes would make me better than I was before. My life must be completely uncompromised, as I was thrilled about being able to do what I wanted without having to confer with anyone. I was pretty self-reliant, as my children were independent, so I could do as I pleased, go on holiday, or even spend my money the way I wanted to. I could feel a sense of peace and calm settling over me, as I did not have to account to anyone about my whereabouts or my actions.

I was queen of my own castle and needed to approach my life with enthusiasm and with a new positive attitude. I refused to put limitations on my plans. The best days were still in front of me. I took pleasure in my time alone and the calm that came along with it. I was starting to let go of the unexpected hurdles that had built up within my heart, and the relief was refreshing. The doom and gloom were slowly fading away.

I contacted my old school friend, Zoe, who was my closest friend from high school since we were fifteen. We were together through our teen years and confided just about everything in our lives, up to sharing our private experiences in the way only best friends do. We grew up from girls to women to getting married, and we even watched our kids running around as infants and growing up to being adults. We'd known each other for over forty years but had grown apart over the last few years. Our friendship had taken a back seat because I was too busy focusing on the hectic schedules of my life. We made arrangements to meet for the weekend. Our get-together ought to be fitting to lighten my mood.

She welcomed me into her home, and we were extremely excited to be in each other's company. It felt like forever since we'd last seen each other. We immediately tried to catch up on the time that we were not in contact. We discussed our most recent events, our kids, our hopes, our dreams, and even our fears. We were both divorced and trying to get back onto our feet. We reminisced about old boyfriends; our schooldays; and, of course, our individual marriages. It was good to be back in the regular world once more, mingling with friends at a different level other than with the kids or friends who did not share the same opinions as me. I missed having her around.

We promised to meet again the following weekend. We felt like youngsters as we planned our fun night out. We settled on going to an uptown piano bar. I hadn't been to a social gathering of this kind in many years, but our excitement to be in each other's company was at a high, even though we were as nervous as a couple of kids. It had been ages since I'd hung out with a friend, let alone enjoyed having a drink. Our get togethers in the past were always hosted at one of our respective homes, either casually sitting around a fire or spending the time indoors.

That night, we had a great time, with lots of company and admirers buying us drinks and coming over to chat with us. I remember freezing as a guy walked towards me. When he addressed me, I could hardly breathe and giggled nervously. He repeated his questions. I managed to nod my head in response. The smile on his face was like an invitation for me to calm down. Deep down, I thought to myself, *Man, this is harder than I imagined.*

After sipping a few glasses of wine, I began to unwind.

My companion lavished all his attention on me, causing me to feel like I was the only important person as we danced and exchanged information about each other. Zoe was also engrossed in conversation with a companion she met. It was a good night.

I slept over at Zoe's place. It must have been the early hours of the morning as the sun was already rising when we eventually settled down to fall asleep. Zoe made breakfast, more like brunch, as it was afternoon by then. We ate at leisure, and then it was time for me to go home. It was good to be getting out of my comfort zone.

The next weekend, we spent the evening together at a different piano bar that had more flair. Once more, we drank wine and danced. I sipped slowly on my drink, enjoying my time out. I slept over at Zoe's place yet again, exchanging stories till the early hours of the morning. This was becoming a habit, and I loved it. We spent the rest of the evening bonding as friends. We exchanged opinions on a variety of subjects. We also learned about the most important things that had happened in our respective lives. We made a promise to each other to never stop having fun because of our age. Instead, we vowed to seek possibilities and use our time constructively. We agreed never to regret anything, or miss out on any opportunities presented to us. We also gave each other all the moral support that we each needed. Having a companion to do fun things with was exactly what I needed to forget my past experiences.

My children noticed the difference in my frame of mind. They urged me to continue enjoying myself and to explore more places. They encouraged our evenings out, suggesting that we were good company for each other.

'Go out more with Zoe, Mom. Meet new people. Make new friends. Don't sit around causing yourself to be miserable,' Colleen insisted. *It appears as if she is giving me permission to go forth and misbehave,* I thought and silently giggled.

I jumped at the opportunity. From there, we met almost every second weekend having great fun and partying like we were twenty. I felt young again, allowing myself to behave freely. I must say we were still very mischievous and as daring as we had been in our youth days. Nothing changed in our prime years.

It so happened that, on one of our nights out, we got carried away and lost track of time. When we looked at our wristwatches, it was way past midnight. We had to walk back to our hotel room, which was about a five-minute walk. As we were strolling in our high heels, we noticed two guys following at a close distance. I vividly remember telling Zoe to run. As we picked up our pace, they also picked up their speed, but we managed to get away. We watched them through the hotel window as they turned around and went back to where they had come from. My heart was beating so fast, and my legs were shaking.

Although it was of a serious matter, we sat flat on the floor in our hotel room, unable to contain ourselves and let out nervous laughter. That was one of the nights we attempted to keep a secret from our kids, but unfortunately, it slipped out during one of our conversations. They were not impressed, especially with the fact that we turned it into a joke and put our lives at risk.

We started exploring different social events, going out for breakfast and doing all that we had missed out on. I started to treasure the perks of my newfound freedom, as I had forgotten what it was like to have fun. I could not remember when last I'd felt so carefree. As I tuned into this vibe of goodness, I found that my confidence was transformed to a feeling that made me feel ten years younger but much wiser. It was good to know that our obligations were less as our lives played out. I was happy for the time spent alone trying to collect my thoughts, even though it was short-lived.

Anthony started phoning with the excuse that he was missing the children. He wanted to know where we were residing. I was determined to be in hiding for a little while longer and did not want to reveal the details of where we were living yet. I was still enjoying my long-deserved break that I needed from anything that would disturb my peace of mind.

After numerous persistent phone calls, there was no way that I could keep the information away from him, as he pleaded, saying that he wanted to spend time with the children and especially the grandchildren. I had no option but to reluctantly give in. I supplied him with the address of the house we were renting. I assumed that he might have eventually tracked us down anyway, as one of our mutual friends may well have probably given the game away and provided him with the information.

He appeared at my doorstep that very same day. The children were very excited to see their father and grandfather. We spent a while in silence, scrutinising each other very uneasily and not sure where to begin. I offered him a cup of coffee as we walked towards the lounge.

After a while he began to spill out his feelings. I made sure that I remained poised and in control.

'I am sorry for all the disappointments and the hurt that I caused you and the children.'

I stood close to the door, listening attentively. I eventually sat down opposite him, aware of the enquiring glances from Robyn and Colleen, which made me uncomfortable; I knew they would not be pleased with my reply.

'I will never do anything to hurt you again.'

The children were all ears waiting for my response, but I asked them to give us our privacy. They reluctantly left their father and me alone so that we could talk.

I worked up the courage to respond to him. I made certain that I chose my words carefully, as I was taken aback by his declaration. I'd imagined that he was coming to spend quality time with the children, not to discuss getting back together.

'It is so strange that all the time that I was right there under your nose, you showed no interest in me. Now that we are divorced, you want it all back. For now, I do not want to discuss getting back together. It will never work. I will always have the image of all these women, especially Avril, in the back of my mind; images don't go away that easily. You are more than welcome to visit the children whenever you feel the need to see them. I will never stand in your way or stop you from seeing them. They are grown up and capable of making their own decisions. As for me, I have started afresh. We can be friends, nothing more.'

'But how are you going to make it on your own?' he insisted.

'You need not worry about me, as I am used to making it on my own. You were always working away, so me being alone with the children is nothing new to us. Ever since I opened my business, you stopped supporting the family, so I have been sustaining myself since then. Please don't ask me for more. I have too much hostility in my heart for the way you treated me in the past.'

He did not interrupt me as I spoke. I made sure that I conveyed my message with the correct tone of voice and that, at the same time, I made my point clear. To my surprise, he accepted and did not pursue the matter further. He seemed more submissive than I'd ever seen him before. Talking was very painful at this stage.

I preferred to change the topic to a more general one. With time the wounds would heal. I was not about to let a bad past ruin my vision for a good future. My concentration for now was the welfare of my family and myself.

A week later, he called again. This time he said he was not about to give up on our broken marriage, insisting that we try again. It seemed, he wanted his family back at all costs. It was strange, as he had always been this tough guy. Yet here he was, begging for forgiveness and another chance. He did not want me back because he loved me; he wanted the security of his old life back. The timing could not have been worse with all that happened in our lives. The fact was, splitting up at our age, also made it a life-altering reality. The idea of retiring and growing old together had come to an abrupt end. We were both required to rearrange our priorities, as well as our future plans.

I remained pleasant towards him throughout the visit, making sure that I put my past feelings aside. Still, an apology at this point could not fix anything, as time could never be returned. Each time I glanced in his direction I noticed how desolate he appeared. His health seemed to have declined; he'd lost weight compared to the last time I'd seen him.

He left with the promise of seeing us the next day. He started to visit and phone more often. When I enquired about his wellbeing on one of his visits, he always had the same answer: 'I feel good. I have my sugar and cholesterol under control.' By now I could sense that the fighting gloves were off. There was a peace that settled between us. The tension diminished.

In the meantime, I was radiant with excitement and looked forward to my weekends with Zoe, as we continued to go out or spend enjoyable time in each other's company, discussing our dreams for our future. We were not prepared to postpone our happiness because we had been knocked down a bit by life and learned a few lessons the hard way.

'Zoe, do you think we will find compatible companions at our age? We are not young anymore you know,' I questioned her on one of our sleepovers.

'We are the perfect age. Each year is special; growing old is a privilege.'

'I suppose it's natural to feel cynical after all the cheating in my marriage, but I need to let go of the anger, for my own sake.'

'The negativity will eventually lessen, Hannah. There are many guys out there who are in the same situation as we are in, looking for companionship. No one wants to spend the rest of their lives alone, unless they choose to. In the aftermath of our divorces, we will be filled with mistrust and negativity, so we may question ourselves and also the people we meet. It will be difficult. We may feel intimidated at first, but with time, our confidence will return,' she assured me.

Deep in my heart, I was not so sure. I thought about my leg with all the scars. All hope left me as I wondered if the appearance of my leg would be acceptable in someone else's eyes. I was forced to deal with the insecurity of being rejected, rather than pretend that the scar did not exist. It was time to stop hiding behind my scars. Leaning on my friend and opening up to her was the support I needed for now.

'Will anyone ever look at me with my leg so badly disfigured and unattractive?' I asked with worry as I pointed to my leg and felt my stomach coil as I explored my feelings of uncertainty.

'If he loves you, he won't even look at your leg. That should be the least of your worries. There are some people who don't even *have* legs. They have managed to lead a full life. You have a lot to be grateful for. Someone who is sincere will look at you as a whole person and appreciate all you have to offer.' Zoe tried to console me.

'I am going to take one day at a time. I promised myself that I will not rush blindly into a relationship with anyone because of my insecurities. When the time is right, whatever is meant to be will happen. I know my leg will not matter to the right man. He would have to be a very special person,' I mused.

We discussed our expectations, not wanting to repeat the same mistakes that we'd made in our past. By the time we parted company, my heart was lighter. I was at peace. Our chat settled me emotionally; moreover, it imparted good feelings to me. I would think of my leg as different, not damaged or scarred. The word 'different' sat better with me.

Anthony's visits became more frequent. We saw him almost every second day. His excuse was still that he wanted to spend time with the grandchildren, and he was concerned that they may forget him. The kids also went around to his place more often to spend time with him. Each time I saw him, his appearance seemed to have gotten worse. He wore a troubled look on his face that told me that something was out of place. I was compelled to enquire about his health once again, but with a forced smile he insisted that he was feeling healthy and in good shape. I could sense that something was not right. I felt pity for him. His health was deteriorating. He implied that he'd stopped taking his diabetic medication, even though he was aware of the implications and that it was not conducive to his health. I warned him that his stubbornness could result in even more severe consequences. I also cautioned him that he was in danger of possible side effects by stopping his medication.

On another visit, he unexpectedly asked me if I remembered our life together and the time we first met.

'It seems like yesterday,' I recalled.

We continued to speak about the happier days we'd spent together and the time when the kids were born. We pondered on their childhood days to their maturing stages.

'What are your plans for the future?' he asked.

'I have not made any plans for my future yet. I've lived through too many changes in the past few months. I'd rather pay my attention to the now than to where I am going. I want to learn from all my errors and try to build something good from the pieces that are left of my life. I think there has been a lesson for both of us.'

I took a moment to peer into my troubled thoughts to uncover the cause or even the reason for the affairs he'd had, but my self-inspection came up with no immediate answers. I had stayed well past the sell-by date in a marriage that was long over. I would continue making mistakes in my future, but they would be different from my past errors, as I had learnt valuable lessons from them. I'd have to be dumb to go back and make the same mistake.

He mentioned that he no longer had the patience to cope with the commotion of his landlord. He was restless, as the living set-up had become intolerable for him. He was unhappy with his current living arrangements and wanted to find new accommodation.

Two months later he moved into Stephanie's house. I offered to help him move, but he declined my offer. By the time the weekend arrived, he was comfortably settled into Stephanie's home. I was relieved that he'd moved in with Stephanie and her family, as she promised to keep a watchful eye on him. She would be able to monitor his medication and administer it to him as prescribed if he was prepared to change his mind and start taking it.

He continued to plead for reconciliation. He wanted his life back, despite the rumours that I kept hearing of him badmouthing me to anyone who was prepared to listen. My answer remained unchanged. Unfortunately, his actions were in contrast to what he was pleading for.

'I am not ready to go back to the life of unhappiness I lived when we were together. I don't want any type of complication in my life anymore. It's good that we are friends for the sake of the children and that we remain civil towards each other.'

I struggled with the gossip people were spreading, though. His gossip went to the extent of telling his family and friends that, because of my influence, his children didn't want to have anything to do with him. *How was that possible, as they spent plenty of time in each other's company?* There was not much that I could do about his instability.

I approached him about the gossips that were circulating, but it was of no use, as he denied all the allegations. My name was roaming out there on people's lips. I found his lies and gossip annoying. His friends and family looked at me accusingly, as if I was to blame for the divorce. One of his family members even had the audacity to comment that I was old and that I should have stayed married instead of divorcing him. Imagine! Did he think that I did not deserve a better life of my own?

Let them judge me, I reasoned. *Their opinions are not my problem to worry about.* People are callous to the pain of others. I concluded that, no matter what they said about me, I would not doubt my worth. If this was his way of letting go of the anger, then so be it. His reactions were expected but uncalled for, as I was forced to live with the hearsay.

Fortunately for me, I did not have to answer to anyone. Above all, he was a grown man who knew the difference between good and bad manners. He had a funny way of trying to make things right. But under the stress he was going through, it was logical in a strange way. I was saddened by his unusual manners, but I did not lose heart by his deception, as the blame must eventually fade away. My option was to suck it up for now. Even though he was sincerely apologetic and wanted to reconcile with me, he continued to interact with Avril, in the hope of making up with her. His actions were nothing short of another insult to my intelligence. He was crazier than I imagined.

I vividly remember asking Anthony, when we were still married, if he still loved me. His response brought tears to my eyes, as he'd responded with aggravation in his voice that I should stop asking him nonsense. But at the same time, he'd avoided the question. At that moment, it had been clear that the love was gone. I should have acted on it then.

The Christmas season was quickly approaching. Where had the time gone? All the shops were decorated with trees and filled with toys and gifts. The days leading to Christmas were insanely hectic, with shopping for gifts and clothing for the children. Everywhere I looked, people were in a festive spirit. I suddenly started to dread the season, which seemed like a useless round of mingling and entertaining.

The season also stirred a horrible memory for me that I was struggling to get rid of from my mind. We attended an annual Christmas party at Anthony's company where he worked. I made sure that I looked my best. I went out of my way with my outfit, which was very expensive. It was an elaborate evening, with everyone looking stunning in evening gowns and evening attire. There was also free-flowing alcohol, as well as other beverages.

The evening went off well until it was time to go home. Anthony insisted that it was still early. I told him that most of the people were gone and that we should go too. He was not ready to leave, and then he turned his back to me and continued to flirt with the woman who he'd spent most of the evening with.

We were one of the last people to leave. As we reached the car, he got crazy and started hitting me hard on the back of my head saying that I'd embarrassed him in front of his colleagues by stating that it was time to go home. I put my arms over my face to protect it from being hit. He then pulled on my dress, ripping it down the middle. He continued to hit me multiple times. I managed to free myself from his grip and started to run in the direction of where there were cars, but he chased me and caught up with me. He pulled me by my dress. By now I was half naked as he pushed me into the car and then continued to punch me all the way home.

Afterwards, it became a blur. He continued to scream at me as we entered our home. The children awoke from his screaming. All three of my daughters began to hit him from all sides. At that point, he backed off. I couldn't comprehend what had happened. Everyone went to bed, as I remained in the lounge. I sat on the floor and cried for a long time. This was one of the most emotionally distressing events I'd experienced, and it was difficult to erase from my mind over this period.

I tried my best to forget this image. I was startled back to reality as the wind blew the door shut.

This was my first Christmas as a single woman. My house would not be crowded. Every year, I stood till my back ached, making the perfect meal, decorating the house for the family, and entertaining until the early hours of the morning. I did not have to prepare a big family meal, as my children planned to divide their time between their father and me. I intended to keep the tradition as simple as possible, preferring to be more laid-back this time. I did not have any intention of putting up our tree, but the kids convinced me otherwise. I anticipated that the holidays were going to be tough with the changes, but I would overcome it. It would get easier with time, even though, for now, it made me miserable. I'd never thought it possible to be spending Christmas without Anthony. The joyful ritual took an unusual turn, with me spending Christmas Eve on my own. Amazingly, I enjoyed the time alone and watched a family movie.

At the last minute, Stephanie invited us over for Christmas lunch. I did not expect Anthony to spend Christmas without his family around him. It was the time of year for family, a time when the family got soaked up in each other's company and exchanged gifts. It was really not what I planned, as I'd already prepared myself emotionally to make a fresh start.

The grandchildren arrived with their parents after midnight. It was difficult getting them to sleep that night when they returned from their respective outings, as they were anxiously eyeing the tree to see if their gifts were there. Robyn told them that, if they were not asleep by the time Father Christmas came by our house, he would see the activity and move on to the next house. That got them to bed quicker than I thought.

Christmas arrived. We all woke up bright and early. The kids headed straight for their gifts. We were not extravagant with gifts this year and tried to keep it low-key, but the kids were happy that Santa had arrived at our house with the gifts that they'd asked for in their letters.

My day started by attending church. I sat down in the pew, listening to the sermon. The words were inspiring, and my spirits were lifted. I had not been to church in a while, not because I'd lost faith but because of the anger I carried around with me. I got the impression that God had abandoned me because of all my trials.

I must say, though, it felt good as I drove back home. I promised myself that I would attend church more often. I was at peace, with renewed strength. I appreciated that I had so much to be thankful for. I began to feel guilty for taking my blessings for granted.

We enjoyed our Christmas lunch with traditional stuffed turkey, gammon, roast potatoes, pastas, and all the other trimmings.

The food was delicious, followed by many different extravagant desserts, not forgetting the Christmas pudding. Basically, we spent the day satisfying ourselves with all the provisions laid before us. I sipped slowly on champagne and then later savored a glass of wine to loosen up.

Because of the tension being thick in the air, Anthony and I exchanged very few words, but we managed to be polite to one another. The day was successful, with lots of laughter and listening to Frank Sinatra in the background. As the day turned into evening, the thick atmosphere lessened. The Christmas spirit filled the house as I listened to the children's playful voices.

In my mind, this was a new chapter. Christmas would be different in the future. New rituals would be created for me. My family traditions were likely to change as time went on. I looked forward to introducing new traditions into my life.

Colleen and Robyn planned to leave home in the near future and would get married eventually. I would have to face those changes that I was dreading when the time came. For now, I would also stop over thinking and enjoy the present moment. I knew we could not count on being together every year. At least it was all behind me; the day ended up being pleasant. I was glad to be back home in my own company as the others stayed behind to enjoy the rest of the evening, confirming they'd be home later. There was a welcoming silence that greeted me. I was thankful for the unrelenting strength that permitted me to face the day; there were no regrets.

The following day was spent at home lazing around, nibbling on the leftovers all day long with friends and family in and out of the house. Everything around me became quiet as I waited for the first day of the New Year to arrive. I became secluded as my daughters went out on New Year's Eve. As ridiculous as it may sound, I was forced to look to myself for company. I started talking to myself and found it weird. At this point, I understood the chilling truth about the real meaning of being alone; it was terrifying.

New Year's Day we celebrated outdoors accompanied by family as we watched breathtaking firework displays, creating loud cracker explosions. The resorts and pools were busy with activity, as everyone wanted to start the New Year near the water. We later had a barbeque for lunch. I did not make any resolutions, as I knew that the chances of my sticking to them were low. The day turned out perfect and complete.

17

With Christmas and New Year's behind us, we soon fell back into our normal routines. The days became less hectic. The bustle of the past weeks ended as the holidays drew to a close. Not all days were good, as each day brought its own challenges, and this particular day was no exception to the rule. There was a major violation of my outlook of the way the world should be and the way my world had become, more challenging than ever before. There were days when I thought I was free from all my difficulties, only to find myself back in the depths of misery, nursing my fragile emotions.

Colleen, Robyn, and I, were still unemployed. We had to scramble for every cent. It was becoming more devastating. My ability to cope seemed to be shrinking. I wanted to understand it all, but nothing was making sense anymore. I prayed every day, without losing hope that some miracle would become visible. My battle was real. Backing down from prayer was not an option for me, as the reward of prayer is great. That night, as I knelt down to say my prayers, I said these words out loud:

'Dear Lord, I thank you for directing my steps today and blessing me with another day. You know the difficult times I have been dealing with. I feel unsettled and concerned about

what is going to happen to us next. Please lighten my burdens for me. I may not understand how everything will work out, but I trust you. Help me to focus on my blessing. Things look dark and black now, but I have faith and trust in your goodness. I am sorry for complaining about my circumstances, but assist me to take it one day at a time.'

I knew that God would never leave me, but my situation was making me lose hope. My life was becoming a frightening place. I was scared about my future. Maybe I would wake up and observe that it was all a bad dream.

Now that the accident was slowly becoming part of my past, I had a new experience to deal with on this journey called life. At the rate it was going, we might lose our rented house, which was in arrears. It was not easy; in fact, it was horrendous. I could no longer grasp the confusion, as I watched myself hit rock bottom. I was extremely vulnerable, as all my expectations that I'd designed for my life were shattered. The money we'd received from the sale of our house was not sufficient to cover all our expenses that we incurred.

I flinched at the thought of letting go of more of my sentimental items, but along the way, I understood how pointless it was to keep them if they were not being utilised; if they could help us to survive through the week, they had to go. They were accumulating dust in storage anyway. My world was not about to end because I no longer owned those goods. Strangely, it also felt pretty good to let them go, as it made me aware that having a pile of possessions was not that important if we needed funds more.

By now, we'd disposed most of our assets on the market to survive through our daily lives. As the expression goes, 'be willing to walk alone. Many who started with you will not finish with you.' I now knew that was a true phrase. The more I thought about who could assist me in my trials, the more I noticed that not one name came to mind. Instead, family started hounding me for money that was owed to them. Family and friends were avoiding us like a plague. I was in trouble. I was alone. Loyalty was so rare.

I chose not to allow the desertion of family to shatter me.

Sadness weighed me down as I grieved for my past. I kept asking myself, *Where did I go wrong? What did I do that was so misguided, for me to go through this terrible patch in my life now?* Maybe I'd made reckless financial mistakes or even bad judgements that were coming back to haunt me.

I came up with no answers or solutions. I was unable to connect the dots to see the bigger picture and to reach a conclusion. We remained positive, as we tried to see the good in each day, thus moving along to more pressing issues. There was no way we could survive without money. Everything we needed required money. I knew what it was like to be in need and what it was like to have more than enough. I concluded that money is a necessity to survive from day to day. It plays an important role, as it enables us to have a comfortable life.

I had a feeling of being submerged in the deepest ocean. We were struggling to keep our heads above water. I was determined to swim out of my situation with all the strength I possessed.

Even though it was a dark time, I was thankful for the fact that I was alive; for all the blessings that were given to me. I did not want to lose sight of what was important, that being the welfare of my family. The best evidence of God's care, was my life itself, the fact that we were healthy and there was a roof over our head, we had warmth, food and we were blessed with love. We learnt to be satisfied with what we were granted.

What was the use of complaining? I reasoned that pitfalls were a part of life that equipped me to deal with any future hardships, while preparing me for inevitable setbacks.

Jessica, a friend I'd met in my working career, was one of the few people who frequently checked up on me, making sure that the kids and I were coping. I received a phone call or a visit from her almost every week because she worried about me. She also provided the necessary encouragement I needed. She was the kind of friend who tried to 'fix' me by putting all my broken pieces together, hoping to remove the instability that was taking place in my life. She offered lots of emotional support and always reminded me of how strong I was. She was a good listener, allowing me to pour my heart out. In addition, she was a positive influence on me, inspiring me to move on. On the odd occasion, we went out for a cup of coffee and spent the day together.

Cassie, whom I met through Anthony, also spent many days trying to console me in an effort to improve my confidence. In our early years of marriage, we endured many trials as our husbands visited the local bars, while we were left alone at home to take care of the children. Once in a while, she would sleep over at my house, providing companionship for me. I valued her friendship, as she made me feel hopeful when she prayed with me. She was a dedicated Christian. I could be myself around her, without pretending to be someone else or feigning that none of this was taking place.

I reflected on our last conversation. 'Negative thoughts spoken out loud are given life. Never speak about the problem but, rather, look forward to God's promises. The world will not stop spinning just because you have a problem, so change your outlook to a more encouraging attitude and always put God first in everything.' I found her advice comforting.

Finally, in answer to our prayers, Robyn landed a job in the insurance industry. Even though the salary she was offered was not what she anticipated, as she'd completed her degree, she was grateful anyway. Our life was not perfect, but we were thankful for what we received, as half a loaf was better than none. There was hope that Robyn would look for better opportunities once she was settled in her position.

Today was a good day for most. There was so much to be excited about. Couples were celebrating Valentine's Day, spending a romantic day in each other's company with red roses and candlelit dinners and a rainbow of joy in their hearts. It was a romantic day for all those who were in a relationship. Happy couples were holding hands and smiling at each other, while I wallowed in my misery. This time around, I had a problem with this day. I uncovered fault in every way possible as to why this day should not exist, as it opened up wounds in me that were healing and the fact that I was alone. I was not in the best frame of mind. Being a social butterfly was not on my agenda. My plan was to have a shower and then an early night so that I could avoid hearing about the beautiful day everyone enjoyed. I was silently nursing my wounds. Watching a movie would just make it worse because only love stories were on the screen and that would make me feel worse about my position.

I received a text message from Anthony wishing me happy Valentine's Day. But my new rule was simple. I chose to ignore it, as I did not want to encourage him in any way. At the same time, I hoped that he would not be annoyed by my silence.

Anthony looked frailer on his next visit. I studied him from across the room where I was sitting. I couldn't help but wonder what the problem was. When I questioned him about his health, he insisted that he'd caught a flu bug and that his sugar was under control. I somehow did not believe him, as I noticed that he was breathing with difficulty, his eyes were sunken, and besides, he looked frail. There was a serious flaw in his body movements that seemed sluggish.

'Stay away from me if you have the flu,' I teased.

A week went by. He only popped in once, which I found to be unusual. The children kept in touch with him by phoning him regularly to make sure that he was doing well and that he was not in need of anything. They undertook to repair any gaps that were in their relationship with their father by going over to his place as often as possible. A lot of effort was put into strengthening their connection. They nurtured their time spent together, taking an active role to maintain the bond after the breakup of our marriage.

On Monday morning, Stephanie phoned to tell me that Anthony had slept the whole day on Sunday without eating for two days. I could sense that she was panicking by the sound of her voice. I phoned him to enquire how he was feeling.

'Like a truck has run over my body,' he mumbled with a feeble voice.

I insisted that he consult a doctor. I promised to accompany him the next morning. I became aware that he must be feeling very sick when he agreed immediately, without arguing like he normally did.

The following day, we met at the doctor's rooms as we arranged. He appeared physically run down; something was very wrong.

'Are you all right? You look extremely pale?' I whispered with great concern.

He nodded as if talking was an effort. His breathing was coming in short pants, as if he was in pain. The doctors ran tests on him and found keratin in his kidney.

'What does this mean?' I asked the doctor. 'Is the kidney failing?'

Questions began to flood my mind. I began to reach unwarranted conclusions, anticipating the worst. The doctor responded that it was not a good sign but expressed that he was to be put on a drip to flush the kidney out. He was admitted into a ward, where he spent a few hours on a drip. He was later discharged with instructions from the doctor to go for more blood tests at the laboratories the following day.

We went through to Stephanie's house that evening to see if he was feeling any better. I made him a pot of soup, as he needed to have something solid to eat. When we arrived, I warmed the soup, insisting that he eat at least a portion of it. He struggled to get part of it down.

The kids were very concerned about him. They spent the whole visit sitting on the bed next to him, in an effort to make him feel better. He found it difficult to stay awake, drifting in and out of sleep until it was time for us to leave. Stephanie was very uncomfortable with the fact that he did not want to go to hospital that evening.

The following day, he went for blood tests. He was accompanied by Aaron. When he returned home, he slept the whole day without eating again. I phoned him throughout the day, checking up on how he was feeling. There was no improvement, and he complained that he was feeling worse. I undertook to take him to the hospital very early the following morning. Once more, he agreed.

That night I found it impossible to get rest. I lay awake, my mind running wildly all over the place. I tossed and turned for hours, believing that he will be healed, but worried that something might happen to him in the course of the night. I was wakeful with a new level of dependence, believing that God was always faithful. I comforted myself that night as I prayed for Anthony's divine healing. The night stretched out, as thoughts of what could go wrong with him filled my mind, weighing heavily upon me.

We'd walked down many roads together and I longed to make this right, but it was not in my hands. I did not know what to do. Nor did I have an idea on how to handle his condition. All I saw ahead of me was a road filled with despair as I thought of the fact that he'd stopped taking his medication.

I called him early the following morning to make sure that he was ready for the hospital. He replied that he needed to take a shower, and by the time I arrived to pick him up, he would be ready. In the meantime, I called his best friend Daniel, requesting that he accompany us. I was afraid that something drastic might happen on the way, as Anthony's voice sounded weak. But Daniel was unavailable to take off work, so I was forced to go on my own.

I phoned Anthony after a while to notify him that I was on my way, but my grandson Aaron—who was twelve years old at the time—answered his phone. I heard his cry of terror as he took my call.

'I don't know what is wrong with my grandad, but he collapsed and is lying on the floor and is not moving. Please hurry!' He sounded terrified as he sobbed and relayed the details to me.

Without giving it a thought, I slammed the phone down. I yelled to Colleen to get ready, as her father had collapsed, and we needed to rush through to him right away. The drive to Stephanie's house was a blur to me. My heart was racing. We kept driving at a high speed, desperate to be at his side. My mind was clouded by my panic.

Within minutes, we arrived at Stephanie's house. It was already too late. We did not make it in time. As I saw him sprawled on the floor, I began to sob, almost tripping over my feet. Pulling myself together, I felt for a pulse. But there was nothing. I shook him by the shoulders, but there was still no response. He was not breathing. I stared at him, hoping for a slight movement. I was totally unprepared to accept that his life was over.

I began to close his eyes, and I grasped the truth that he was deceased. *Why did I have to delay?* I fell on my knees. I knelt beside him, feeling his body; it was still warm. If only I had been given some sort of warning to come within the hour to have a brief moment to say goodbye.

We lifted his lifeless body and then laid him down onto the bed with the help of Aaron, Colleen, and the helper. I learnt that, when he fell, he'd hit his head against the wall. There was a gash at the back of his head. Bending over his unresponsive body, I dressed him with a shirt before everyone arrived. Thereafter, I covered him with a blanket.

The next few minutes were foggy to me. I vaguely remember phoning Stephanie and Robyn to let them know that their father had passed away. Colleen and I phoned the respective families and friends to inform them of his passing on. It was difficult for them to believe this information of his passing on. The words were difficult enough to come out as I called to inform those who were close to him. I sobbed uncontrollably, and my hands were shaking. My voice was frantic; I was scared out of my wits as I spoke into the phone.

'*Dead*? How can that be? What happened? He was fine last week. It's impossible,' everyone said in different ways.

I was unable to answer the many questions put to me. Like them all, I was also desperate to understand, even though, deep down in my heart, I knew that he'd stopped taking his medication for his diabetes and continued to live his life as though the illness was not there. I tried to reconstruct the events from all his visits that could give me a clue of what led to his death, but I found nothing that could have prevented it. If only I'd predicted earlier that he was seriously ill, I could have been able to take preventive action. But I'd taken it for granted that he was suffering with a flu virus like he'd informed me he was. I was emotionally shocked by the sudden loss. I was especially sorry for my children, for their grief that was still to follow.

The house filled up with people, as relatives and friends were there in a matter of a few minutes. I sat beside his body for a long time, blaming him for his death. I could not deal with one more catastrophe. My cup was over full; I had more than enough, more than I could handle. My burdens were becoming heavier to bear.

My life was falling apart. There was no way of escape, as I thought of all the heart-wrenching misfortunes I had been through. I could not fight against the injustice that was taking place in my life any longer. Like prey being savaged by a predator, I was being hunted down by this injustice.

'Why did you have to resort to drinking so much? Why did you stop looking after yourself? What went so wrong?' I demanded from him, full of rage.

I shut my eyes hoping the grief may ease, expecting some answers to all my questions. I left his side and focused on my breathing. Nothing was worse than what I was experiencing.

'Why are they taking so long to move his body?' I put the question to William.

I was advised that there was a delay because all the family members needed to view the body before it could be taken away to the mortuary. William took control of the situation, as I was in no state to make any decisions. Anthony's body remained on the bed for over three hours. It was beginning to get stiff and letting off a slight smell, or maybe that was in my head. We all surrounded the bed to say a prayer. The children remained at his side, speaking privately with their father before he was moved and struggling to bring their connection to a positive end.

William gave instructions to the undertakers to remove the body and informed those who hadn't seen his body that they could view it at the church. I watched as his body was taken away.

He was truly gone for good. I pulled myself together as I stepped outside for a breath of fresh air. I looked around me and noticed that family members and friends were grouped together speaking in soft tones. Many people arrived to pay their respects.

'My deepest condolences,' or, 'I am sorry for your loss.'

I was without emotion as each one whispered in my ear. My mind ceased to function; their words ended up sounding like a recording. I sat back and observed everyone as they came. I was horrified as I listened to their accusing assumptions and harsh comments. I heard loudly whispered remarks saying, 'The divorce killed him. Why did she choose to divorce him now? She is the cause of his death because she accepted his affairs in the past. Why did she abandon him in his time of need? She left him when he fell seriously ill with no one else to turn to. Her vows of sickness and health meant nothing to her.'

Their statements were extremely predictable. Surely, they could have waited a day or two. In a way, the people making them were hoping to push my button to see my reaction. Yet, if I had seen it coming, why was I horrified? At one stage, I felt like yelling at them all, but I managed to remain calm. Responding to any remarks was definitely inappropriate at a time like this. Their timing was so wrong. People needed to have something to say. I could not prevent them from putting their thoughtless views forward. Maybe it was their way of easing the pain that they were feeling?

I needed to proceed with caution around such toxic people, as this was just the beginning of a long, ugly journey. I did not have the power to utter a word to defend myself or even to protest to any of their remarks. I was a suspect in a murder case—what a tragic scenario. Sometimes, it is a blessing to have annoying people around because it helped to give me an indication of what to expect by being around them. I chose to become alert to their scornful remarks and, at the same time, learn to manage my emotions. I preferred to set the tone for how this would unfold by remaining composed. I comforted myself, knowing that God's grace would be sufficient for now.

Raven seated himself on the chair next to me and raised the question with regard to the funds for the funeral. 'Do you have any burial insurance?'

I did not appreciate the conversation at this stage, as Anthony's death was still fresh in my mind. Can *this not wait for a more suitable moment when there are fewer people around? I considered.* 'Not nearly enough to cover everything,' I answered him anyway, as the question was bound to come up at some point.

He was aware of my financial situation. One of the insurance policies had lapsed, as I was unable to maintain it. But that did leave me with a minor policy that would cover a fraction of the costs but not the full costs.

When the divorce was finalised I'd removed him from most of my policies. William had a trivial policy through his company, but it was not enough to cover the full outlay of the funeral. I had the urge to run, but I couldn't, because it was my responsibility to face what lay ahead no matter how painful it was. Even though I was legally divorced, it seemed like I was obligated to help the children bury him. The hurt was all-consuming. I was at a point of breaking down but had to remain tough for my children.

When Megan and Zoe arrived at Stephanie's house, they immediately spotted me and then came rushing towards me. I was relieved to see them. They embraced me as I shed tears of grief. They assured me that everything was going to be fine. They understood my struggles and offered me genuine compassion. I was fortunate to have them in my life.

'Why is all this happening to me?' I questioned. My mind was worn out from searching for answers. 'Needless to say, he was ill for a long time. He was ill with diabetes and cholesterol. A few years ago, he underwent a triple bypass,' I rattled on, seeking to justify the events of his life. I continued to speak, not waiting for a response from them. 'He was not willing to change his lifestyle. He refused to make the necessary changes for his health. He seemed to have given up hope after the divorce. I don't understand fully because it really was what he wanted.'

My situation was difficult to understand, but I knew, one day, God would reveal why all this had happened this way. Something seemed to die within me as I thought of my children's reaction to the loss of their father. There was a sad paradigm shift of my existence that turned my world upside down with such large alterations to my life all at once. I considered dealing with this shift in my life by adjusting the way I looked at what was happening to me. I would get myself through all this. My reality became tough. I did not see this coming. In this difficult moment, I learned the power of prayer, as it caused my hope to rise above all the pain I was feeling. I was sad, but it was essential that I survive this ordeal.

People were in and out of Stephanie's house. I stared at some of the unfamiliar faces as they arrived. I could not help but wonder who they were and how were they associated with him. The same questions had to be answered over and over. *What was wrong with him? Was he sick? How did he pass on?*

I kept my voice steady as I offered a response to the questions that were directed at me. 'The paramedics diagnosed that he died of a heart attack.' I ought to feel something, but I was numb. His life ended too soon.

I especially felt sorrow for his children as I watched them grieve for the person they loved so dearly. All three of them reacted distinctly by allowing their grief to unfold on their own terms as they worked through their feelings. No matter how difficult the road ahead seemed, I pushed forward. They would never forget their father; I was aware that they would cherish the positive memories about him.

Being the surviving parent, the challenge for providing support to them was great, as I was obligated to process my own grief. He battled for a number of years with the challenging health setbacks in his life, but he lost the fight along the way. My mind continued to drift to its own space. I could not tell yet whether it was heaven or hell. I was still looking for a miracle to happen, but his death was inevitable. The time would come for me to accept it, even though no one prepared me on how to handle the loss of a life, especially that of someone so close. I gathered that death did not happen at our convenience; it must happen sometime or another in everyone's life. I was sucked even deeper into the abyss of my mood as I thought about the funeral planning ahead of me. During this time of loss, I found solitude in seeking God.

18

The family met at Stephanie's house the following morning to map out the funeral arrangements. Anthony's brothers were present, as they'd offered to help financially. For the next few hours, the family was in profound discussions about finalizing the funeral preparations. We discussed the church, made an appointment with the church secretary, who took care of the time of services and set out all the procedures of the ceremony. We met with the undertakers to discuss their part in the handling of the procession of the funeral. We talked about the estimated costs of the coffin, the church, flowers, and the catering. I appointed myself to take charge of the catering, together with Stephanie, Colleen, and Robyn to ensure that the most suitable menu was selected that would meet our needs. At the same time, my mind would be occupied. We all agreed to honour his wish for his body to be cremated.

I was grateful that the meeting went smoothly. The whole process fell into place without any fuss, and I was hoping for a good send-off. When we arrived at the funeral home, I noticed that his family was accommodating to our decisions, even though I was divorced. I decided to take a back seat and leave some of the other choices to them. I offered input when required. His two brothers who had past experience in the planning of a funeral, Raven and Carl, were helpful in guiding us through the process, except where the children had strong feelings on certain issues, such as the flowers, along with the colour scheme. My sister-in law, Emma, who worked in the printing industry, agreed to design the pamphlets, with remarkable results that pleased his daughters.

Our family doctor completed all the forms that were sent to her by the funeral home but, in the process, neglected to sign the most important page. She returned the forms without the required signature needed to obtain the death certificate. I had a very good relationship with my doctor and at this stage she was very sensitive to my needs. By the time the mortician discovered the missing signature, my doctor had set off on holiday and was only due back four days later. The result was that the funeral was delayed for a whole week. It was a sign from above, testing my patience. My sentiments were, the quicker the better; it meant spending more time on Anthony's departure, as though I did not have enough on my plate. The wound would be left open for longer than intended. I wanted him rested where he needed to be, and so did the rest of the family.

Many people presumed that I'd caused the delay of the funeral so that my family could arrive from their various destinations in order for them to attend the funeral. Their theory was nothing but an act of cruelty that was aimed to hurt me. I decided, no more arguments! I would not pay any attention to any more accusations, especially if the blaming was a threat to me. This was a road that I did not choose to be on. I was, once again, presented with a tough situation, which I was more than glad to take up.

On one of the days leading up to the funeral, Shaun implied that Anthony had died of a broken heart due to the divorce, which resulted in people whispering to each other.

I found this remark to be short-sighted and shallow. Caution urged me to ignore his comment. I was relieved when I heard Zoe strike back at Shaun's remark. 'Blame is the easiest and most destructive game to play, as it only makes us feel better about ourselves for a while. Anthony did not die of a broken heart. If your brother had taken care of himself, he would be healthy. It is mean, vindictive, and hurtful to make such strong allegations as to blame someone else for his death. We are all adults sitting here today. Adults take care of themselves; they don't rely on the next person to be healthy. If you need to take medication or have to eat properly, the onus is on you to do so. Your health is your responsibility, not someone else's. I suggest if we need to blame anyone for the things that go wrong in our lives, we need to start with ourselves.'

There was silence as she got up from her seat to catch a breath of fresh air and shake off the feeling of annoyance. I appreciated the fact that there was a good squad behind me. I had the support of my family and friends. I refuse to allow his family to contaminate my aura. If we were holding others accountable for Anthony's failing health, then Shaun was obliged to have advised him to take better care of himself, instead of drinking and partying with him almost every weekend. Shifting the blame on me was an easy way out for him. He wanted to absolve himself from any wrongdoing with regards to Anthony's death. In spite of the fear of being criticised, I would do the right thing and continue to give Anthony the dignified funeral he deserved.

The memorial service took place at my house because we were unable to book any available venues for that particular day, as those available were all unbefitting for the occasion. We kept the procedure light-hearted. After the service, we showed photos on a slideshow in remembrance of Anthony's life. Surprisingly, there were no hurtful episodes on the day, except for the gathering of people in the bathroom making snide remarks, which I totally ignored.

Mourners came to Stephanie's house for the next two days to sympathise with the family. There was laughter, not serenity the way I imagined mourning to be. I presumed Anthony would have liked it the way it was turning out, as they were celebrating the life that he lived in a way. Then again, my idea of sympathizing was different. I was not here to condemn what I was witnessing, though, but merely to help the children to bury their father. Sudden death does not often allow us to say goodbye, so maybe this was one of the ways that some people were declaring their valediction.

Time seemed to fly by. The day of the funeral approached quicker than we anticipated. We awoke early to prepare for the day. When we arrived at the church, my daughters and I assumed our places beside the coffin in the vestibule of the church where it was placed. As everyone arrived, they had easy excess to the viewing of the body before entering the church.

The ceremony began. Judging by the attendance of people present, Anthony had inspired many people in a positive way. He'd lived his life with a passion and was well loved by all who were present. As for me, it was difficult to remember the time when I loved him, but I knew that I had loved him at some point of my life. But I guess it was hard to evoke the moments that marked that point.

The front-row seating in the church was allocated to the immediate family.

I sat in my seat with trembling hands. My eldest sister, Geraldine, sat beside me, comforting me throughout the funeral ceremony. All three of his daughters shed bitter tears during the procedure. The grief was evident in the church as the sound of soft sobbing could be heard all over during the service. Stephanie went forward to share a eulogy in tribute to her father. Raven also did a tribute about their life growing up as children and all the fond memories they shared as a family. Marlon, a school friend, the third person to speak about their schooldays.

After the church ceremony everyone filed out of the church. The body was loaded onto the hearse and then transported to the crematorium. During the cremation, William played one of Anthony's preferred songs, 'Go on and Cry' by Bloodstone.

After the cremation, we drove back to the church hall where the meal was served. The caterers were well prepared. I later learned that the meal was complimented by many people. Most of the day remained hazy to me, as I could not remember some of the things that had taken place on that day or even some of the people who'd attended. I remember glancing in the direction of the people present. Even though we were at a funeral, there was laughter among the groups, which showed the acceptance as each one worked through the startling reality of his death.

Megan, Zoe, Ann, and Jessica comforted me throughout the whole process. There was always someone at my side uttering words of encouragement, while others showed kindness towards me.

Even though it was difficult for some people to choose the appropriate words of comfort to express the sadness they were feeling for my family, it was good having them here at this moment, as we appreciated their support.

On my way out, I bumped into Raven. I walked towards where he was standing to thank him for the assistance they'd provided towards the funeral. He looked the other way and chose not to converse with me. The same attitude applied to the rest of his family. I was uncertain as to why I was being ignored. I stood there for a moment in disbelief, trying to make sense of their conduct, but their intent was unclear. What an unkind attitude at such a sensitive time. This seemed to be the end of our relationship as a family.

Maybe I should count it as a blessing, as I won't have to force myself to be in their company or make false conversations with them, I reflected. I was not sure what I'd done to offend them, but I was more than certain that I was being ignored because the blame for Anthony's death was being shifted onto me.

If only they would look me in the eye to express what they were feeling, instead of ignoring me; it ought to put my mind at rest to know exactly what I had done that was improper and warranted treating me so unfairly. This did not surprise me, as Megan warned me earlier that there might be lots of accusation thrown in my direction. Yet still, I struggled to get my head around what transpired. If they were not prepared to discuss what they were feeling towards me, there was nothing I could do. Their actions were left hanging in the air, with me being held accountable for the loss of their brother. I could not describe the pain I felt, as it all seemed to have gone wrong.

We assembled at Stephanie's house to hold the post-funeral gathering, as it was customary to get together and catch up on family matters after a funeral. There were many relatives that I had not seen in a while. This was a good opportunity to reconnect with them in a more casual atmosphere. I sat in the company of my family as we reminisced about Anthony's life. The conversation was kept light. I could not wait to be home alone to drown in my own wretched mood. I needed time to process all the events in order to accept them.

Back home, I fought back tears of frustration as the reality of it all hit me. I struggled with the acceptance of my situation. My thoughts wrestled with God about all the developments that were pulling me down. I laboured to remain optimistic. At this moment, I was not in a forgiving mood. I held a lot of bitterness in my heart towards Anthony, with the way my life had turned out. But I was no longer going to concentrate on the morbid details.

He had gone to a better place, a problem-free place, where he was free from all his illnesses and the need for any medication. For what it was worth, I did a great job with regard to my contribution to the funeral, including the part I'd played in his life.

With the funeral behind me, it was time to redefine myself and plan for the life I so deeply desired. I did not want to be mad anymore. I was experiencing all kinds of unexpected feelings, but I reasoned that the pain would eventually ease. I was still learning to manage my pain and anger, even though it hurt so much. For now, my life was full of ups and downs. All I had to do was turn the page of my book of life in the right direction and not to get stuck on the page of being afraid, sad, angry, or miserable.

The coming year was going to be filled with challenges for my family. As for me, I would look back on the past few days and observe that I worried too much about things that really didn't matter. Even though we were divorced, we still had thirty-odd years of bittersweet memories of sharing our life together. Those memories did not erase themselves from my life overnight. Instead, I would trust my instinct; if something felt wrong to some degree, then I wouldn't do it. Letting go of my depressing feelings was a key step to moving forward and dealing with the pain of loss. I needed to survive what the world had thrown at me. I elected to avoid any triggers that brought back my past. There were certain feelings of betrayal that I could not control, but it was essential to set the tone for them while I figured out how to advance to my next level.

In the meantime, I kept getting flashbacks of the trauma of my accident that constantly popped into my mind and left me with a feeling of sadness. How ironic, the one thing that connected me to my father robbed me of leading a normal life — the tractor.

I recall my last ride on the tractor with my father before he died. There was something stirring about that particular day. My mother warned him to take precautions during the ride, which he always did. We took a drive to the highest mountain. When we reached the top, we got out and seated ourselves on a comfortable rock. The view was magnificent with the sun setting in the background. We sat in silence admiring the scene; no words were needed. Of course, on the drive back I indulged in talking.

I would not allow the accident to rob me of these memories. My leg would be a constant reminder, but I had to let go of these recollections of the accident. I was grateful that I lived to tell the tale. I had to get back to living a normal life, instead of carrying this worthless baggage about the accident with me wherever I went. It was important for me to get back to my activities, as hard as it seemed. I needed to connect with old acquaintances who would accept the new me. It was time to sort through my thoughts and get rid of the clutter and make space for better things that lay ahead. This applied to people who were weighing me down and did not add value to my life. If somebody could not contribute something good in my life, then I needed to let that person go.

I considered it weird that Anthony would no longer be walking through my front door anymore, yet I knew he would be a constant presence in our lives. When I looked at everyone on the outside, I realised that life goes on as if nothing has changed. One day all this would make sense to me.

There were so many things I'd lost over the past few years but also so many I'd gained, in wisdom and knowledge, that were priceless, as they contributed to my inner growth. I did not understand many things; I did not know what tomorrow would bring for me, but I was at peace. Life happened, but I was thankful for all my blessings. When I look back on my years, I see much suffering, but I also see a glimmer of hope. Everything I held was stripped from me. My world changed. It became distorted. I was forced to let go, but I stood my ground and chose the faithful road.

My life was unclear compared to a few years ago, but that did not mean it was the end. This was the beginning for me. Great things were waiting for me. I would plant my feet firmly to the ground in a sensible way. I'd been through the worst, but no matter what I'd been through, I was still here. And that, in itself, told me that God had a plan for me, and I will stand to His good promises. My storm would die down; I would draw strength from all my ups and downs.

19

It was time to pay attention to the matters that I'd neglected in the past few weeks. I needed to turn my attention to the winding up of Anthony's affairs. Being tough was my only choice, though sad memories kept creeping into my mind. It was difficult to remove them from my thoughts, but I had to because it was senseless, as there was nothing to be gained from dwelling on all that had happened. I had to let the wall down that I had built around myself. It was important for me to keep busy to block out these persistent thoughts. I would start appreciating where I was in my journey as time went by.

My moment to concentrate on me was short-lived. Like a volcano erupting, the worst aspects of the family emerged. There was hearsay that I was in possession of Anthony's car papers. William approached me, affirming that it was Anthony's wish for his car to be transferred into his name, as we were not in a position to maintain the upkeep of the car. In addition to what was happening, Carl became persistent and kept on phoning to enquire about Anthony's possessions.

It was hardly a surprise when, two days later, he again made enquiries as to when Anthony's affairs were expected to be sorted out; he was keen to be present because Anthony owed him money. I informed him that I was aware of the money that was owed to him. As soon as I was financially stable, I took it upon myself to repay him. The weight of the pressure being put on me was crushing me down. It was rather wise not to mull over the reason for their actions.

Carl came knocking on my door on another day, despite the fact that I'd informed him that, as soon as funds became available, I promised to give him a call. He arrived again a week later. I somehow expected him. This time, he enquired about Anthony's car, demanding the keys, as he wanted to make use of it to transport building material. I informed him that the car was already sold.

'You have no right to go about selling his assets or disposing of his possessions, as you are divorced.' I was taken aback by his reaction.

'I can sue you for this.'

'Go ahead. Sue me. I have not sold anything. Feel free to contact his daughters, who are his next of kin and are representing their father. Besides, they have the full authority to dispose of his belongings as they deem fit. I suggest you run your intentions by them.' I remained level-headed, hoping to come out of this with no emotional bruises.

I resented the implications that people were making. Family that was supposed to give me their support became the cause of my stress. Without a doubt, this was not the last that I would be hearing from them.

Two days later, Carl was back, accompanied by his wife. This time, he wanted some of my furniture. What the hell was going on around me? They began to threaten me and became very rowdy, as his wife repeatedly slammed her hand on my furniture, but I chose to remain calm. They were reckless in their actions and did not understand the pain they caused me and my family as they acted out in front of them. I will look back to this moment that brought me to tears.

Some family members, who I never imagined would have conflict over material things, wanted his watch to help them remember him. Another wanted his jackets, someone else wanted his fishing rod, and the list went on. People were opportunistic, and that was just a reality, but I needed to protect myself from them. It became a game of greed, and I had never been exposed to such manners in my entire life. I had a great need to escape the turmoil. I was grieving a death; all people cared about was whatever worldly possessions Anthony owned, because I was divorced, and I was not entitled to them.

It was time to step away from everyone that disturbed my peace. I must remain loyal to myself. Even though my values were under attack, I would continue to live by them and fight back. I would not lose them for the sake of pleasing someone else by reacting to their comments and actions. I had to find a way to step back from the situation.

On the days that followed, there were many more such occurrences. Stephanie contacted Raven to release the boxes that Anthony stored at his house so that the family could sort through his belongings. He refused to even hear about it until he received the money that Anthony owed him. He sent Stephanie very nasty messages relating to the boxes, without thinking of the sentimental and emotional value some of the items had for the children. He would not be able to put a price on some of them. She responded that he could keep everything that he had in storage to avoid starting any new arguments. He reacted by threatening to take us to court, which resulted in both parties in the families bearing a grudge against each other.

It was such an awful thing at this stage of our lives. An already difficult situation became a mess between the two families. I hoped, somewhat in vain, that it wouldn't divide the family further. Instead of the families benefiting from supporting each other, our differences set us a distance apart. We found ourselves at odds over material possessions and money. I was annoyed, judging that Anthony might not be happy with their unethical behaviour.

The reactions to a death make people do unpleasant things and say crazy things. In the case of his family, their true colours were beginning to show. An alien seemed to have invaded our lives, as the actions of everyone around us became unpredictable and confusing. The sad part is, that words once spoken cannot be retracted. I have learned that people will forget what you said but will never forget how you made them feel; right now, they were making me feel really low.

No amount of reasoning could change my mind about how I felt. My emotions were bordering on hatred, which was a strong, ugly word that seldom entered into my word list. Thinking that I could change their actions was a waste of my energy.

To add to my stress, the tales continued, uninterrupted, making their rounds back to me. The rumour mill was more intense, spreading like wildfire. But I reminded myself that the truth was invincible, that even though I was under attack, the facts were more likely to win in the end. I was losing my family too, as they were making false accusations, more revolting than the other tales that surfaced. The tale was that my daughters or I had taken out a policy on him that amounted to a large sum of money.

'Really, my own family fabricating lies?' It rocked me to my core. *Is this normal conduct at such a time as this?* I questioned myself.

The trouble was brewing, revealing a strange turn that was unfamiliar to me. I made every effort to pay no attention to what was being assumed, taking life one day at a time. Yet, I felt terribly let down as I listened to the harsh comments. They created a vision of me that they wanted to believe. I wanted to find a way to forget their malicious gossip. My hope was uprooted, and I was being battered from all sides. I was utterly ridiculed. I was fed up with the talk and needed to understand why I was being discredited in this way. I would own my battles, as there was nothing to hide on my side. I did not have to ask for forgiveness. Nor would I conform to reduce someone else's insecurity. It was clear that these people were dealing with their own shortcomings. I had very little indication of what the solution would be. I would never look at them in the same way again.

The relationship between the families had taken a mysterious turn. I was getting the rotten end of the deal. I concealed a lot of bitterness in my heart for the way everything was turning out.

I was losing my mind. People continued to slander my name. I seriously wanted to filter out my friends and family who did not know my worth. These were the callous after-death issues I was dealing with. I kept telling myself that this was not real; it was just a projection. Gossip of this nature does circulate and usually has a short lifespan. Like a balloon, the tales would float away; tomorrow I will be old news. The reality was people were going to talk, period. I also reflected on all that had happened and knew that things are seldom put back together the way they were before. But somewhere in my mind, I distinguished it would get better.

Megan made time in her busy schedule to make sure that everything was going well for my family after the difficult time we were going through. Her timing was perfect, as I needed someone to talk to. I briefed her on all the incidents that had unfolded over the past few weeks. She was confused by the facts that I put before her.

'Why are you liable for paying his debt if they keep reminding you that you are divorced? Why ask for his car when he has children who are his beneficiaries?' Megan enquired, trying to establish the true motive behind their actions.

'The money he took from his brothers was when we were still together, so clearly I am obligated to pay it back.'

'What did he use the money for?' Megan probed.

'To pay his personal debts and some of the household expenses, as there was no income. Besides the business was doing poorly at the time.'

'Then it makes sense that they would claim the money from you, as you say. My suggestion, though, is for you to pay your portion of the money and get some legal advice with that regard, and if they want all his possessions, make sure you include all his debts,' she simply resolved after giving it some thought.

'I just want to pay the debt and get them off my back,' I said urgently. 'Death really brings out the nastiest qualities in some people. It seems as if there are those who thrive on the weaknesses of others who are at their lowest point. Now I know what it feels like to be a victim.'

'The past few years have been very eventful for you. Everything hit you at once. You faced struggle after struggle, with many strange things happening in your life. But nevertheless, just remember that a butterfly only appears after a caterpillar has gone through its transformation. All you can do is transform with your struggles.' Megan comforted me, looking very concerned for me.

'I know. All I wanted was a divorce and to be away from the cheating and, above all, the lies. But instead, I got much more than I bargained for.'

Megan seemed a distance away; she hesitated, wanting to say something but stopping herself, and walked over to stare through the window.

'It is difficult to respect or even like people for what they have done, because their actions will keep coming to my mind even when all this is over.'

I explained that I needed to forgive them for *me*, so that I could move on with my life.

'I have lost everything I ever worked for, but I did it once, and with my unrelenting prayers I will do it again. I will overcome this battle.'

We said our goodbyes and went our separate ways. The funny thing about all this is that I am no longer angry, even though it still hurts a lot at times. My emotional state was extremely delicate and sensitive, but I promised myself that there would be no more tears. I would put on my happy face and smile at the world.

As this day comes to an end, I reflected yet again on my many blessings, even though the ruthless events kept rewinding in my mind. Over these past few days, I'd witnessed how the game was played. I personally learnt to stand firm while playing the game fairly, irrespective of the outcome. I matured and was more 'armed' to accept my fate. The situation also helped me to come to terms with my circumstances and enabled me to grow in the right direction.

The debts that were left behind needed to be straightened out. I could not saddle the children with this task. I started by phoning the debtors and then sent them the required documentation that they requested to conclude the debts off Anthony's name.

Once that was done, it was the right moment to sort out his belongings. The girls agreed, and they set time aside on one of the weekends ahead. We began by sorting out his clothing, tools, and personal effects. Some of the more sentimental items were kept by the children. The rest of the items were set aside and boxed. Some of them were donated to the church. I was thankful that there was harmony all round. Moreover, we were on the same page as we bundled his belongings and made jokes about certain outfits to keep the atmosphere light.

It touched my heart as I glanced at the girls concluding the job at hand in a gentle way. My family bonded at this stage. I was glad that it was becoming easier, even though his death had a profound impact on their lives. However, the sadness would come in stages. I trusted that they would push through the low times. It was depressing to think that this process may possibly have to be repeated as soon as Raven changed his self-seeking attitude and decided to part with the rest of Anthony's possessions; if not, we agreed that he could keep everything.

Throughout my life, there have been hard times. I have trained myself to use these difficult times as life lessons. This was one of those lessons that was teaching me to get my power back. I would not be obsessed or controlled by material goods, even if they had sentimental value to me. They were not that important. I searched deep in the archives of my mind to find the key to my grief. I had to forgive. *If I don't forgive, it will eat me up*, I reasoned. For years, I'd endured the hurt and lived with blame in my heart, but these would not last forever; they never do. My train of thought would change and become different once forgiveness set in. My growth towards forgiveness would help my healing; nothing would defeat me. I resolved that things that caused me to go down would not change who I am.

The sorrow was taking a long time to end. It was very painful for me and the girls. This final step of letting go was also part of the grieving process. Grief seemed to have drained me. I seemed to be doing things more aimlessly than was normal for me. It came to mind that I was accountable to respect his last cremation wishes, which were sacred to the girls, to scatter his ashes and say our final goodbyes. We concluded that the ocean would be his final resting place, as he requested. At the same time, the family made a decision to take a much-deserved break from all that had happened and wind down.

We opted for a beach that we often frequented for our holidays to carry out the scattering of the cremated ashes. This was to be our ultimate connection—the final symbol connecting us emotionally.

We chose an isolated spot on the beach to perform our final act of respect. The waters were alive as the wind blew the waves towards us. I tasted the salt on my lips. We included blue flower petals, which was his favoured colour, in tribute of his memory.

When we walked far enough into the ocean, we opened the wooden box and slowly spread the ashes along with the petals over the waters. I had never done this before; for a minute I wanted to be elsewhere. Nothing prepared me for the intense compassion I felt as I watched the ash land on the ocean and then drift away as if carrying him off to a peaceful place. It was difficult to imagine that someone could be reduced to a few handfuls of grey powder.

It was a sacred image to absorb. Robyn took great pride in capturing the precious moment on video. I hoped that the images would give some comfort to the children when they viewed these pictures and the video when remembering this day.

I remained staring at the picture of the ocean as the waves lashed against the rocks. I marveled at the wonderful sight before me. We kept the event as simple as possible.

When the deed was completed, we headed back to our holiday house. Once again, few tears were shed; instead, we shared some pleasant memories of his life. The atmosphere was calm, and the heaviness was lifted off my shoulders until Colleen enquired of her sisters, 'Who is going to walk me down the aisle when I get married?' My heart was broken all over again as her words stuck in my mind. There was no response as we all stared at her, not knowing how to react.

I suggested counselling with a professional for the family when we returned home. Seeking help at this stage could only result in some good for each one of us. It was essential for the family to be prepared to deal with the image of what the scattering of the ashes left behind and the unpleasant incidents that had taken place over the past few weeks. My thoughts processed the reality of the loss, as I resolved to constantly pray for serenity.

With the funeral, the cremation, and the disposal of his belongings behind me, I had the urge to scream for joy with relief. It was time for me to say goodbye to my past. I did not know how, but I believed in myself. When I looked back on my years and thought of all the pain that I have endured, I couldn't help but also see how much God had richly blessed me. I would fight the good fight to the end and wear my crown of victory with dignity. I'd kept my faith thus far and would continue to let time heal all my painful memories. I knew that I would cry at random times, but that was to be expected. I would look at the world in a different light, where everything felt right and I was at peace with where I'd been and to where I was headed. Nearly everything that could go wrong has gone wrong. Nothing could possibly go wrong anymore.

20

eeks turned into months. The memories of my trials became evident in my body, as I remained exhausted. My life was not a fairy tale, but I started to regain my self-confidence. I looked forward to the changes that I planned for my days ahead. It was not a good idea to sit around moping indefinitely. I'd stopped living in my past. I trusted my judgement as I made my decision to start afresh. It was going to be stimulating to revive my life and rid myself of all the havoc that had somehow become part of me.

The voice within me reminded me that the end of my struggles was finally in sight. My future was not as dark as I'd envisaged. I began to face life with a more positive attitude by looking for the best in everything. I would fight to get my life back, and nothing would derail my happiness again.

To our relief, Colleen managed to find employment. She became very excited as she went through her wardrobe, figuring out on what to wear for her first day. I was happy for her, as she'd become restless being at home for such an extended period of time.

It was a new undertaking for her, and the sparkle in her smile put me in harmony.

Zoe invited me over to her house on Friday evening. I showered and paid particular attention to my appearance. I applied my make-up with extra care. I went to the hairstylist during the week to have my hair done. I was given a trendy haircut, which looked good on me, as it enhanced my features and made me feel young. I did not compromise on my outfit, which was a simple pair of jeans with a fashionable summer top. The combination boosted my confidence. It was time to pause and channel my energy into building something new that could benefit my life.

Zoe and I sat in the living room discussing our plans on where to go to for that evening. It felt good to be anticipating my new life as we sipped our drinks, listened to music, danced, and discussed our prospective venue. Listening to the words of a song by Elton John, *'I'm Still Standing'*, made me feel like a survivor and gave me the opportunity to take a good look at where I was. I'd faced the chaos head-on and lived to tell the tale. Having weathered many storms, I was inspired to have survived all my emotional upheavals.

Zoe and I imitated every word with enthusiasm as we danced and felt exhilarated. It was a pity that I'd cut myself off from the social life. Due to my ignorance, I could not come up with any interesting ideas of where to go, as I had not been out in a while.

If I went out on girl's night like most normal people did, I would have come up with at least a few places we could visit.

'The game is going to be trickier at our age, but I do intend to have fun and get back on track. I am sure many things have changed over the years, but the principles should still be the same,' I said rather nervously, as I was without a clue about where people spent their leisure time other than the places we'd visited recently on our outings.

'We need to keep up with current events so that we don't lose touch with what is going on around us. But where to start? And where do we go? We need to go in a different direction, not to a piano bar,' Zoe pointed out.

'I have not socialised at this level in a long time. There are so many new social gathering places. The options are numerous. They all look appealing; hence, it is difficult to decide. I read a comment that experts say that we should embrace technology.

Maybe we can start by registering on one of the online dating sites, as research shows that it is the best way to meet new people in our age group,' I suggested. Perhaps it was time for me to broaden my circle and put myself out there, and then I might find companionship.

'Been there, done that. It did not work out for me,' said Zoe.

It took us some time to find our bearings. We eventually settled on going to a dinner club. It was a social networking venue that encouraged single people to meet and have a pleasant evening in a relaxed environment. The ceiling of the venue was low and gave the place an intimate atmosphere. Our dinner was delicious.

We had a few drinks, danced, and listened to soft music in the background. We mingled, but I concentrated more on getting acquainted with the feeling of being out again. We made many friends that night, and we exchanged telephone numbers. We stayed for a few hours, and then we called it a night.

The following weekend, we met again and sat around listening to music along with sipping on our wine before we agreed to go yet again to another piano bar called Hollywood.

It was a lot easier finding a venue this time, from our previous searches online during the week.

Upon arrival, we were ushered to a table. There was a dim lantern burning in the middle, giving off a warm glow. The setting was decorative, bearing a resemblance to the eighties. Whatever happens tonight, we knew that it was going to be good. The band entertaining us that evening was awesome. They played various types of great music that featured a blend of hip-hop and other irresistible dance beats that lured the crowd to the dance floor. We were confident in ourselves, expecting to blend in, as we were talented dancers with rhythm. We were thrilled that we remembered most of the lyrics and could sing along. There was a chilled-out vibe there; it was a place anyone could imagine themselves to be in.

The crowd became more vibrant as the evening wore on. We loved the excitement and the energy. Once during the evening, I leaned back in my seat and exhaled all the negative energy out of me, planning to soak up every good moment and thinking that this could really grow on me. The good life began here — right now; I was at peace and loving my present.

We noticed that the crowd was younger than we'd expected — not really what we were hoping for. I swallowed my drink and really appreciated the taste; it made me feel restful. Zoe swirled her glass of gin and tonic in her hand as we watched everyone dancing, while others sipped on their drinks.

'I hoped to see more mature guys in the crowd,' I remarked. But at the same time, it wasn't a big deal.

Zoe nodded in agreement, as the music was too loud for me to hear anything, and our words were drowned by the noise. I was bubbling with excitement when a group of very fine-looking men walked into the room. I guessed they were between forty-eight and fifty-five. They appeared unruffled and were out to have a good time. The dancing became more alive as the dance floor filled up. Just then, I turned my head and stared into the most approving smile, which belonged to one of the men who'd just arrived.

'Is this seat taken?' he posed the question in a soft, husky voice. Before I could respond, he sat on the chair beside me with his drink in his hand, and leaning in closer, he began to converse with me. He was looking at me like I was the most important person in the room.

I could not respond as my heart jumped to my throat. I shook my head in response as he continued to speak to me with a flirtatious smile. I nodded my head in response. Zoe kicked my leg under the table to jerk me out of my awkwardness, and then I began to speak. It was crazy, as I was as nervous as a teenager.

His closeness was freaking me out. I did not realise that meeting someone could be this complicated, as I became withdrawn and selectively social. I sensed his warm gaze analysing my face as he introduced himself, and his smile deepened. I managed to give him my name and even muttered a few words.

We continued our conversation more easily as the evening advanced. He put many questions to me and also shared some of his opinions. His laugh matched his smile; my discomfort eventually ebbed away. I began to relax. What's more, I owned the space around me, hoping to make a lasting impression. I somehow kept him captivated. Flinging all qualms to the wind, we danced and drank all night long. We also exchanged telephone numbers, promising to keep in touch.

The night did not turn out that badly after all. In fact, it turned out fabulous, I mused, and was satisfied that I'd handled meeting the man with no difficulty. This was my possibility; it was time for me to courageously pursue my happiness. We enjoyed every minute of the evening. I'd been out of the dating game for a long time. It was time to brush up on my social cues, and for the first time, I thought I could do it and might even consider dating again.

I slept over again at Zoe's place. We spoke about the evening's events until the early hours of the morning. I could not contain the sensation of happiness that I felt as we looked back on our night out. The morning light streamed in through the window, marking the dawning of a new day, but we were too exhausted from dancing all night to notice.

I slept more peacefully these days. I woke up to the aroma of brunch cooking. With great effort, we got out of bed and made our way to the kitchen, where Zoe's daughter, Kim, prepared food for us. After having our meal, we walked down memory lane, chatting about our lives, as well as confiding in each other about our past experiences.

We lazed around for most part of the morning. We giggled as we discussed our days at boarding school and all the strange incidents we'd landed ourselves in. We were always willing to take risks to make our lives interesting. We'd been caught many times and then disciplined by our superiors, as we were full of mischief back in the day. We also discussed the idea of planning a boat cruise, which was high on our agenda. It was something we both felt we could really look forward to as our highlight for the future, so we put it on our bucket lists.

I arrived home later that afternoon and jumped into a bubble bath, and thereafter, I relaxed in front of the television. My muscles ached, as I was no longer as fit as I used to be. I needed to get back into shape and considered joining the gym. I promised to live unconditionally and to chase a life of peace. As I'd grown older, I was finding that true happiness did not come with a price tag but comes from deep within.

The following days went by pleasantly without any unusual events occurring. I was absorbing every ounce of contentment. On this particular morning, I woke up refreshed with a smile on my face. I was inspired as I sat in front of my computer, with my coffee in my hand. I opened my mailbox like I did every morning to check on any new developments. I blinked my eyes as I read an email from a company I'd applied to for a contract to perform a project, six months earlier. I had been awarded the contract to supply consumables of a very high quality! The work would be performed over the next three years. The company was looking for a long-term vendor. We were chosen over many other companies that had applied.

I sat in front of my computer for over an hour, just thanking God. I was delighted to be granted this opportunity and looked forward to working as part of this team. I was filled with excitement as I picked up the phone to broadcast the news to my daughters.

They were just as excited for me as I was. When I put the receiver down, it suddenly hit me like a blow to my head. It was impossible to carry out this project with absolutely no capital or no machinery. I sat in silence thinking about how to execute this project. I needed a miracle. I was put under great pressure as my mind went wild, thinking that this venture was impossible. My elation at the news of the contract was short-lived, as my self-doubt came flooding back. I did not know how to fix this. My world was crashing around me. That familiar yet provoking pang of distress was back.

My dreams were disrupted. I found myself dealing with unnecessary issues, like where would I get money or even machinery for the project? I did not have business premises to operate from. Such issues were taking up my valuable time instead of allowing me to respond to the good news I received. I was caught up in a grueling depression, desperate to find a solution. I tossed and turned during the night, thinking that there was no way I could build my business with no capital or resources!

The days dragged by as I walked around aimlessly, sweating for two solid weeks. I prayed every minute that I could. I knew God would never give me such a project without the means of fulfilling it.

By the end of the second week, a miracle *did* happen. I received a call from my attorney, Viola, who informed me that my case with the Fund was finally concluded after six tedious years of waiting and many delays. Compensation for my accident was decisively settled. I breathed a sigh of relief, not knowing whether I should cry or jump for joy. My case had taken forever, with many unresolved investigations, but my lawyer had stood firm to get the best settlement for my proceedings. She was not about to settle for less and had won the litigation better than we expected. I could not help but smile with relief at the outcome, as my confidence returned and I wanted to celebrate. It was time to rearrange my plans.

What are the chances that both doors opened at the same time? The timing was beyond words. *This* was what was meant by 'God's time'. Often, I felt that my life was falling apart, but in fact it was falling into place. That road was not always smooth. I found out that waiting is a given. Although during my time of waiting, my faith was stretched to the limit. I put my trust in the One who knows everything. When I think of my future, I am encouraged.

The availability of capital from the fund, together with my policy that had matured, meant that it was time to move ahead and bring my business back to life. The maturing of my policy had totally slipped my mind with all that was going on around me. My struggles had come to an end. I could barely believe that this was taking place, as I'd waited so long and lost all hope. I placed the unprofitable bad memories behind me, permitting my intelligence to direct me. It all felt right, I was stimulated to know that I was on the path to restore what I'd lost.

I loved this adjustment of independence very much, as it began to grow on me almost immediately. The idea of being my own boss again was motivating, as I was a keen businesswoman. I was pleased to be getting back into the driver's seat and taking back the opportunity to be the entrepreneur I once was. I truly believed in myself. There was no better time than now to take control my own destiny. I was so ready for this. Almost four solid years had gone by of being idle. I could not compensate for the lost time, but I could learn from my past.

I found new business premises and planned to be officially operational within the next three weeks. This time, I purchased the premises instead of renting them. I rounded up my old team. We were thrilled to be working together again. Colleen resigned from her company and was excited to join me. It did not take long to restart my business, as I was self-sufficient with the necessary experience. We worked day and night paying great attention to detail, ensuring that every object was in place.

By the end of the three weeks, we were ready for production. The reopening went off smoothly, with everything falling into place as predicted. This was going to be the beginning of a successful mission. It was time for me to do something more lucrative than ever before. Being a business owner was no walk in the park, but I owed it to myself to make it a success. I had a positive mental attitude; this time, it could potentially be for keeps. I was going to be fearless about the challenges in my life, as I was physiologically tougher, and I was geared up to accomplish more than before. I'd gained many life-changing experiences and had learned many lessons in my past; one of them was never to lose hope. I did not only want to be good, I wanted to be the best that I could be. The last few days were mentally draining but, at the same time, very inspiring and evidently worth every moment. It was time to go out there and try out new projects.

I managed to expand my horizons by securing two more large contracts. I centred my attention on the second chance, certainly with the renewed hope that God gave me. I concentrated on all the miracles that were happening in my life.

The desire to have closure and finally letting go of that horrific day lured Megan and myself back to the scene of the accident. We stood at the spot where the accident had taken place. I was terrified as I looked at the steepness of the hill. I had the urge to run back to the car to escape from the memory. My whole system wanted to shut down. I sat very still on a rock, clasping my hands together to keep them from quivering. We sat still for two hours, saying very little but avoiding the exchange of words, trying to accept what happened. I closed my eyes, and a replay of the moment flashed before me like it was taking place now. I caught Megan glancing in my direction a few times but avoided any contact. We made our way back to the car and drove off in silence. Maybe I would deal with the pain and stop avoiding visions from the accident after confronting that fateful day.

Some time passed, and I woke up bright and early to meet with Megan. We went out for dinner; this time our visit together was tranquil.

'I'm going to watch you become financially liberated. You did it before; you can do it again. This time you can do it better by making the best of the present moment in building your business, creating success, and achieving your targets,' Megan whispered, with a bright smile on her face.

'I am confident that this time it will be exceptional. I am beyond certain that it will be a success. I made every effort to achieve a favorable outcome. When I look back on all my struggles, I see now that I have grown from each and every challenging time.'

'I know you will be happy with the way things have turned out in your business, as well as your life. All the unpleasant experiences are behind you. You are at a point in your life where you have reconciled with your past. You have won the battle, I can see the happiness in your smile. Things are working out for you. Your struggles were not in vain because they have given you wisdom.' Megan sighed, reaching for my hand.

'For the first time in years, I feel at peace. I have this sense of relief that it will be okay. I will constantly aim to improve the business. I will not rest on my laurels and take things for granted like I did in the past because everything is running smoothly.'

'Rome was not built in a day. It will all fall into place. I am so happy that it has turned out positively for you, Hannah.'

'I know! I have decreed that I will put my happiness first. The last few days have been incredible, with everything falling into place. You know what is so amazing about all this is that the fear of failure that I've been carrying around with me is now all gone. I just have this new feeling of peace with so much happiness and a completely new attitude.'

'You deserve happiness and nothing less!' I was blown away by my new confidence that came gushing over me as Megan supported me.

'I wonder if the feud they have against me will end. I don't want to walk around knowing someone out there has something against me. I could not bear the thought of shouldering a grudge. It is a horrible feeling to indulge in resentment, as it will eat me up inside. It is so much easier to resolve your dilemma. Maybe I also do have a share of the blame for my broken marriage?'

'Are you talking about your ex-in-laws? They have their own lives to live; don't worry too much about them. They may come around, but at the end of the day, you did no harm to any of them. Forget all the problems, as dwelling on them will rob you from leading a fulfilling life. I know things have been tough; there will still be turmoil from time to time. But that will eventually leave you as you become more confident. Do not seek approval from anyone, as you will become disenchanted in trying to conform to people who you've outgrown. You answer to one person; remember that. As for your marriage, you know deep in your heart that you did the best you could.'

'Why were my trials so profuse? Why did they all come at once? Why me? Why did this happen to me? Could my problems not have been spaced out? I got the impression that God abandoned me along the way and forgot about me.' I started to question God's presence, but I knew his faithfulness was indisputable.

'You were chosen because you are a strong woman. Not once did God forget you. He carried you all the way when you were at your lowest. That's why you are where you are today. You did not give up on God because He had a special purpose for you. Do you remember your mother's words? *"Pray until something happens"?'*

'I do remember her words; Robyn reminded me about them the other day. I do pray every day. I thought I was going to have a nervous breakdown at one stage, but this was the life that was destined for me. My life seemed like God was giving me a story to tell. I have faith that my story will end with an incredible life filled with joy, one of those 'happily ever after' found in a romantic book or one of those successful stories.' I will fight and run my race to the end. I was optimistic about our conversation and confident that everything would turn out for the best. Megan made me see that life was filled with unexpected stumbles, to look at my times of being knocked down as learning lessons and to keep going.

One thing I did learn about prayer is that, as long as I remained faithful, it was a step in the right direction. And it was the most powerful weapon given to me to use against my problems and for my spiritual passage.

21

My journey had taught me to start appreciating things in a different way, never taking anything for granted. I should not have to face a life full of ups and downs or a life-threatening moment to appreciate what I was given. My mindset told me that what I already acquired was sufficient to make my dreams come true.

Everything was taken from my life, but circumstances allowed me to stand firm. Where faith and hope grow, miracles happen. I was not broken beyond repair; on the contrary, I'd become a tougher person with the ability to move forward with confidence and learn from where I'd failed. I was in control of my existence. I would wear my scars proudly because they had taught me that I was a fighter, and I would not be defeated. I would get through whatever life put before me by making good choices that would bring me gratification.

Circumstances could change in a heartbeat. My circumstances changed overnight, I was different; I'd rather follow respect and do what is right than take a shortcut that could bring me pain and suffering.

'Will you consider marriage again Hannah?' asked Zoe as we sat at a table across from each other in a coffee bar, sipping on our milkshakes.

'I hope to consider marriage one day, although in some respects, I think marriage is overrated; been there done that.

It may lead to divorce again. I am not ready to be in that place called love yet. I thought my marriage was solid but look where it ended up. At this point, I like my life the way it is. I do not need any distractions. I need all my time and energy to pay attention to my business.' At this instant I was doubtful about commitment to anyone.

'Not everyone is the same. You may just find someone who is caring. The perfect person will come into your life at the perfect time. You will understand why nothing before now has worked out, because all the pains equally with your miscalculations were simply a platform that was preparing you for better. Think carefully about each and every choice before you make a final decision.'

'I know, it will happen when the right moment comes, but at this stage, I want to play it safe. When I look at my reflection in the mirror, I don't see that young girl anymore. I've past my prime years. All I see are wrinkles on my skin, but I also see a more tenacious person looking back at me.'

'Those are lines of wisdom telling your life's journey. We all go through difficult times with disappointments. Right now, there is a positive change taking place in your life, and you are leaping back into a better position. There are unpleasant incidents that take place in our lives that break us, but they also mature us so that we can become steady and grow to be better people,' Zoe said, emphasising the final phrase about growth.

'I don't think we have aged that badly, you know. However, having a companion does make sense, as it can become very lonely sometimes. I do crave company — someone who will be loyal and respect me. It will make a difference to have somebody to explore and go on adventures with, maybe company to go out to dinner with or someone to watch a movie with. There is so much I still want to do. I plan to travel—but not on my own. A partner may well be a benefit. I want to be happy. I want my head cleared of all the horrible memories. I do not foresee myself going through life on my own. Being alone does not feel right. I may consider it if I meet the right person. Let's see how it plays out.' I still felt very skeptical.

'Give yourself time. It will happen. Concentrate on your present life, not the one you left behind,' advised Zoe.

At that moment, I had a flashback from my past as I heard a nearby dog bark. I was taken back to my time in hospital; my body tensed. The flashback was intense as I saw the dog come towards me. I began to shift in my chair. After a terrifying twenty seconds, I began to relax.

Zoe looked confused as the little dog came towards us to make friends.

That was just a reminder of where I was. We continued to discuss our future plans. Zoe promised to make the necessary arrangements for our boat trip before we parted.

'Everything happens for a reason!' This is an expression I hear all too often. I was striving to look deeply into this aphorism to find the encouraging side that related to my situation. Maybe I'd made too many wrong choices along the way and had reaped the consequences. My anxiety once more peaked as I thought about the condition of my leg; would any one look at me with all the scars on my leg?

I subconsciously began to rub my leg and reflected on Zoe's words that I could have corrective surgery. Technology had advanced over the years, and my leg could perhaps be made to look almost the same as the other one. My leg had recovered well enough to do everything that the other leg could do. It was time to let go of all the human concerns and simply find the inner sense to concentrate on all the good that had come out of all this.

Just to think that not one bone in my body was broken with a weight of plus or minus 9,000 kilograms that was on top of me! It got me reasoning that life is fragile, and nothing in this world is guaranteed. I was blessed beyond measure to be living a normal life.

I quickly came to the conclusion that my ability was far stronger than my disability. After our conversation, I found acceptance. The only thing remaining was the skin graft. Life had given me an obstacle, and I would work with it to overcome the challenge.

I considered all the tragedies in my life to be gifts because I was taught big lessons that changed me. My life would never be put back together the way it was before. It was time to leave the past behind. The thought that I might not be able to dress in a certain way was devastating to me though. I wanted acceptance for the way my leg looked, but there was no point in crying over what suitable clothes to wear but, rather, I should adapt to my situation and not expect the situation to adapt to me.

Recalling my ten-year-old grandson, Cooper's, words while we were shopping put a smile to my face. 'If someone stares at your leg, Ma, tell them to take a picture; it will last longer. So, buy a short dress, I give you permission to wear it.' To make him happy, I bought the dress even though I knew deep in my heart that I would never wear it.

If it were not for my faith and the help of my Creator, I would not be standing here today. I am happy to be where I am. Everything that happened in my life was intended for the best, even though it did not appear so at the time, and I will be forever grateful. My positive approach was going to have a big impact on my quality of life and that of my family. I was on cloud nine, and I was flying without wings. My passion for life was on a new high.

I promised to take it one day at a time. I did not know where my life was going to go from here, but I will fight back and push hard till I get to where I needed to be. I was only too willing to embrace any opportunities that might lie ahead and bask in my serenity.

We all adjusted to our new roles in life. God had greater plans for me. I didn't yet know which way He wanted me to go, but He would reveal it in an unexpected way. I did not know what His revelations were, but I knew that they will be special because His plans are good, these thoughts kept me going.

'Come see our new home. Let me show you around,' Alexa, my granddaughter, yelled with excitement. This was my new home, my new life. It was one of the happiest moments given to me.

I remembered the days when I used to dream about being in my own home again. It was no longer a dream but a reality. I was super-excited. I could not put into words how great this feeling was that I had made it this far. I would no longer answer to fear. Nor would I be frightened about what comes next, as a whole new world was waiting for me. Everything had worked out just the way I wanted it to. I was at the starting point of the rest of my life. I was well on my way to fulfilling my dreams. Every day brought me a step closer to my goal. I did not feel too badly with the way my life was turning out. My arms were wide open to let every moment in. Mistakes are the building blocks of wisdom, they say. It is very true.

The wind was whistling outside as I sipped my coffee. Darkness had fallen. I walked out and stood on my balcony. I looked up at the sky and noticed that the clouds were low-lying with a storm quickly emerging. I could smell the rain approaching as the wind blew the fresh aroma of the damp earth towards me. The lightning blazed in the sky, lighting up the space around me, and the thunder rumbled. A gusty wind blew towards me as the trees swayed in all directions. Within minutes the rain began to pour down, causing water rivulets in the garden.

The sound of the rain pelting down was calming and reminded me of my childhood days. I made a small fire in the fireplace. Within an instant, my room became warm. I sat in my favourite chair in front of the glowing fire, basking in the luminous hearth. I watched the flames change colour as they flickered and leaped about; the outside cold melted away. I made a light dinner of chicken salad and settled into bed to read a book.

Unable to concentrate on the book before me, I stared into space, distracted once more, my heart pounding as I remembered the extent of my new relationship.

Zoe and I had agreed to spend a Saturday afternoon in a park that we regularly visited. It was a warm afternoon as I sat on the bench waiting for my friend to arrive. I did not put any effort into my appearance that particular day. Scanning the park, I caught sight of a figure of medium height who had just entered the park. My hand immediately brushed my hair in an effort to tidy it. I held my breath as he came closer. My eyes glanced at his left finger, trying to see for any signs of a pledge on his side. I found that there was none.

The stranger sat next to me on the bench. He glanced in my direction and smiled. I simply returned the gesture and then continued to look in the direction of the entrance. I could not concentrate on anything with him so close. He seemed very confident as he struck up a conversation about the weather. Five minutes later we found ourselves deep in conversation. We were very comfortable in each other's company, as if we had known each other for a long time.

Just then Zoe appeared with a big grin on her face as she looked at my companion. I reluctantly stood up to leave and find a cozy spot where we would spend the day.

I happened to bump into the man I met while waiting for Zoe, at the café in the park and we continued our conversation for a while. As we were about to leave, he handed me a serviette with his name and number and a message saying, 'Text me soon.'

The relationship developed very rapidly from there. The rest is history. I tried my best to resist at the beginning, but I found myself falling for his exquisite charm. He did not seem in the least concerned with the scars on my leg. I despised regrets and decided to be honest with my inner feelings. I gave in to his influence.

I agreed without hesitation to his proposal to be engaged. We were dating for only six months, and the thought was scary, as this was a big step for me. I had grown accustomed to being alone. It was time to forget that there was sadness in my life. My mind returned to my book, but I could not concentrate, as my thoughts kept drifting to their own place.

The rain stopped. The feeling of spring was in the air; everything outside looked fresh; the plants appeared radiantly new. The scene seemed to be implying that I was being given the opportunity of a renewed purpose, and I was being nudged forward to take the risk that would benefit my life, but at the same time not wanting to rush the process of marriage yet.

At this stage, marriage was a big step and I preferred waiting before taking the leap and making sure that they were for the right reasons.

My cheerful mood told me that I should travel more, go to cinemas more, dine out, and spend more time with my family. I committed to take more long walks and long baths. I would invite my family over for lunch on Sunday and cook a well-deserved meal. We would spend quality time in each other's company. It was time to introduce them to my companion. I could not wait to see the expressions on their faces. I smiled as I became aware of each one's individual reaction but nevertheless hoped that they would accept him. For some unspoken reason, we'd delayed the meeting of the respective families for as long as possible.

I had a sudden longing to be home with my parents, to sit at the foot of their bed and have a heart-to-heart like I had when I was little or when I was troubled. My heart yearned to hear my mother's soothing voice, as well as my father giving me all the guidance I needed to understand this complex world I was living in.

I thank God every day for His unconditional love. Life is full of give and take. I have learnt to give thanks and to take nothing for granted. Each passing day put more distance between me and my trials, together with the horrific memories that were slowly starting to fade away. I would get there.

I had transformed to the person I wanted to be, and was proud of where I was. I'd come to terms with what had happened to me. I'd dealt with everything that had hit me in my life. I was at peace with my past. I am still learning to be kind to myself. If I had the power to turn the clock back to do it differently, I would choose not to, because my experiences had taught me lessons that made me who I am today.

The fact is, that no one can turn the clock back. I started to become a vessel of healing and inspiration for individuals around me. If anyone can benefit from my experiences, then the anguish was worth it. God allows us to go through hard times. I waited patiently for His answers. I did not put my hope in things that might deceive me. Even when my situation was bleak, it was my faith and prayer that carried me through.

It will be my turn to tell people to have hope. What's more I won't just be saying it, but I will be living it. God is in the midst of my situation and is greater than my problems. Praying became my source of help and solace.

A Note for My Readers

I hope you have enjoyed reading this book and have found it inspiring. My book teaches us to hold on and never to give up, no matter what our situation is. We are all surrounded by troubles that are just emotional burdens that weigh us down. Give up the things that weigh you down; don't carry a load that we cannot handle.

Too often, we tend to nurture and carry negative memories of hurt and anger. Why do we allow these to untidy our lives? There are much better thoughts to live with, which are happy and uplifting.

If you want to be happy, never dwell in the past. Let it go; release the past and the failures and embrace the present. When life gets difficult, it is easy to throw in the towel; don't do that. Sometimes the pain was so hard to bear, giving up was the easy way out, but it was not an option for me. Many times, I believed that it was the end, but my journey continued and shaped me for the better because each day of my life is a picture that I will never see again.

Remember the things you have faced and the battles you have won and all the fears you have overcome, the times you have doubted yourself, but you overcame the doubt. Remove doubt from yourself because *you* are the driver of your own life; don't let anyone steal your seat. No one is responsible for your happiness, but you yourself. To stand alone does not mean you *are* alone. I questioned on many occasions through my difficult journey, *Where is God?* He was there all the time through my trials.

'He will never leave you, nor will He forsake you.' These are powerful and very true words of a promise, so remember them. I managed to let them grow on me. Life has taught me a great deal, and the most important thing it has taught me is to trust God in good and bad situations. Only He can turn any situation around, and He is always faithful to His word. My journey is proof that God was walking with me all the time. I have come out stronger than I was before, stronger in my life, stronger in my thoughts, and stronger in my faith. We have one life, and we are given only a tiny opportunity of valuable time on earth. Never think that you have lost time because it took each situation to bring you to your present day. The best decision I made, was to appreciate each day and use it intelligently and never to let yesterday's failures and pains ruin the beauty of the moment. Let every day be filled with love, faith, and hope. I had come too far to settle for second best; I was not born to be second best. Someone once said at a wedding I attended, 'You are so poor; all you have is money.' Money is the worst discovery humans ever made; yet it is the most trusted and desirable thing because it makes our lives comfortable. Identify the value of things and teach your children to do the same.

I have stopped worrying about what I have lost or even the people I have lost. Those people who are meant to be in my life are with me, and as far as those who are not in my life, their absence has made me a better person. Walk away from people and thoughts that undermine your peace of mind or poison your soul. Choose to be the good person in secret. Don't get discouraged, no matter what your situation is because all prayers are answered — sometimes not in the time or the way we ask, but according to the will and the time of God.

Prayer is the key because it changes our joys into blessings and our struggles into new hope. I have accepted myself the way I am. I am no longer a slave to my thoughts of fear, terror, anxiety, or defeat. Nor am I afraid of the unknown. I no longer react to unpleasant or emotional situations. I trust God and Pray until Something Happens. As we run and finish our race that is marked out for us, let us envision hearing people rallying us on as we have a new vigor and motivation to keep going with Faith.

About the Author

Mother of three. Had various occupations but spent most of my career in the insurance industry focusing in Human Resources.

My preferred being an entrepreneur in the Agri food industry. I am Registered as a qualified assessor within the training sector.

When I am not working, I read a wide variety of books and watch some sport like tennis and soccer. Love adventure and any kind of challenge. I recently started exploring art. A slogan that resonates in me is 'I see trials as probabilities and struggles as an opportunity to develop your strength.' I am a Survivor when disaster strikes.